MUDDY WATERS

MUDDY WATERS

An Insider's View
of North American Native Spirituality

NANCI DES GERLAISE

LIGHTHOUSE TRAILS PUBLISHING
EUREKA, MONTANA

Muddy Waters

2nd Expanded Edition by Lighthouse Trails Publishing; 2nd Printing 2015
1st Edition 2008, Pleasant Word

Lighthouse Trails Publishing, LLC
P.O. Box 908
Eureka, Montana 59917
www.lighthousetrails.com

Scripture quotations are taken from the *King James Version.*

Thank you to Richard and Linda Nathan from Logos Word Designs, Inc., for their contribution to the book: www.logosword.com. Cover design and book layout by Lighthouse Trails Publishing. Cover photos from www.bigstockphoto.com, used with permission.

Library of Congress Cataloging-in-Publication Data

Des Gerlaise, Nanci.
Muddy waters : an insider's view of North American Native spirituality / Nanci Des Gerlaise. -- 2nd expanded ed.
p. cm.
Includes bibliographical references.
ISBN 978-0-9846366-4-8 (pbk. : alk. paper)
1. Indians of North America--Religion. 2. Healers--North America . 3. Shamans--North America. 4. Des Gerlaise, Nanci. 5. Indians of North America--Biography. I. Title.
E98.R3D445 2012
299.7--dc23

2012012635

Printed in the United States of America.

Contents

Note from the Publisher

As we began preparing this book for publication, we realized the sensitive nature of publishing a book like this. First, we ourselves are not Native American or First Nations, so some may ask, what gives us the right to publish a book about Native Spirituality? As white Americans and born-again Christians, we are very aware of and absolutely against the prejudices and the injustices that the U.S. Native American and Canadian First Nations people have experienced. While reading this new edition of *Muddy Waters*, we learned of the residential schools in Canada and the boarding schools in the U.S. We were appalled to learn how the young Native children were taken from their parents' homes then placed in these schools and subjected to physical, sexual, and/or mental abuse.

When we traveled across Montana and Alberta in 1997, it was the first time we had seen any of the reservations. From what we saw, it was obvious the Native people had been short-changed in the land they were given by the U.S. and Canadian governments. It became clear to us the reservations weren't faring too well. We later learned of the high suicide, alcoholism, drug, and other abuse rates found on the reservations. Our hearts went out to the Native American people whom we saw as the forgotten people of North America. Yet, we didn't know how we could possibly help. Little did we know back in 1997 that we would start a Christian publishing house in 2002; little did we know that we would later publish our chief editor David Dombrowski's favorite book (next to the Bible)—Egerton Ryerson Young's book from the late 1800s, *Stories From Indian Wigwams and Northern Campfires*; and little did we know that we would stumble across Nanci Des Gerlaise.

We offer this book with the utmost humility and gratefulness to the Lord for giving us the opportunity to publish a book by a Cree First Nations Canadian woman. We pray the message in this book will be received by both Native and non-Native people and that it will cause many to be set free by the only One who can set man free.

To all the missionaries who have selflessly and lovingly given of their time in obedience to God's command: Go ye into all the world, and preach the gospel to every creature. (Mark 16:15)

A Cree Camp in 1871 in Alberta, Canada

PREFACE

I wrote and self-published the first edition of *Muddy Waters* in 2008. When Lighthouse Trails Publishing came across the book and read it in 2011, they approached me, asking if they could publish a new expanded 2nd edition. I saw this as an open door to reach even more people with the message in this book.

The original edition of *Muddy Waters* is about one-third the size of this new edition. What is different? First, I have added four biographical chapters. I also added two chapters regarding how Native Spirituality and some current trends (such as the Indigenous People's Movement and the Emergent Church) coincide with one another. All in all, this edition has six new chapters, two new appendixes, and a name and topic index.

Many Christians see no problem combining the beliefs and practices of Native American Spirituality with their view of Christianity. This book was written to assist such believers who do not understand the subtle snares of the devil and Christ's call to complete holiness and truth. Like them, I ignorantly engaged in Native Spirituality without prior assessment of the spiritual consequences of this false worship.

Yet, this book is also written for non-believers who are struggling with many problems, such as family, substance abuse, health problems, and the darkness and evil of this world. Do you have peace about your spirituality and your spiritual heritage? Does it fill the emptiness in your heart? What is your assurance based on? Do you know where you will go when you die? Are you certain you can stand before divine judgment?

Perhaps like me, you too have encountered problems with your background of North American Native Spirituality. You've lived some or all of a mixture of Native spiritism, Roman Catholicism, paganism, and Christianity all of your life. Perhaps you haven't questioned it before now, yet something about it has been disturbing you.

This book offers you the good news that liberty is available for you through the risen Lord Jesus Christ. Do not be afraid, there is hope! A hope found only in Jesus Christ. It is He who freed me from Satan's prison—He can do the same for you. The choice is yours.

This book is for those who may be suffering, as I once did, from the results of involvement in demonic activities, without understanding what they are. Maybe you have been struggling for years. You know something is very wrong.

There is an answer.

Read on.

Author's Note: My own name, the names of living family members and relatives, and the names of some places have been changed to fictitious ones to protect my own privacy and the privacy of my family.

ONE

A MEDICINE MAN'S DAUGHTER

"The daily effects this kind of influence had on our family were tremendous. It was a strange and difficult childhood, full of hard work, abuse, neglect, and alcoholism."

The darkness clutched me like a shroud, alive with evil, poking, prodding, whispering and hissing its unmistakable message: Fear. Slavery. Terror. Death. Buried under my blanket, I held my breath, with my eyes squeezed shut, while my chest became taut with fear like the skin on the drum the medicine men pounded. Around me, the house lay all too quiet, while the muted sounds of the forest, with its hoots, chirrups, and rustling magnified my fear.

How can my family rest so peacefully? I wondered for the thousandth time. *Don't they feel this evil presence? Am I the only one?*

As long as I'd lived, it had always been there. I popped another sleeping pill and waited for its calming effects to set in. But I had been taking too many, and they were losing their effect. In desperation, I popped a third one, gulping it down with water, and waited for the blessed unconsciousness to hit.

Such was my life from the time I was a young adult until I was almost forty years old.

++++++++++++

I was born in the late 1950s into a family of sixteen children on a Métis Settlement in Alberta, Canada. My family descended from a long line of medicine men, which included both my Grandpa John and my dad. Often, the two spent time in the sweat lodge praying for healing, guidance, or whatever they needed. Our home always seemed filled with a dark evil presence that created havoc during the day and crippled me with fear at night. The objects Grandpa and Papa kept had demonic spirits "attached" to them, like the medicine bundle, the sacred pipes, the "protection" (from evil spirits), and other similar items. Grandpa John used to make "protection" for all of his descendants, which he gave us when we turned eighteen. This "protection" was merely a fetish sewn inside a leather pouch with either a leather throng to wear around the neck or waist, or a safety pin to pin on clothing.

Grandpa also used to make voodoo dolls, asking me to cut pictures of people out of magazines. I have a sneaking suspicion he used their pictures for the faces of the voodoo dolls, because he used to laugh about it when I asked him why he wanted the pictures.

The daily effects this kind of influence had on our family were tremendous. It was a strange and difficult childhood, full of hard work, abuse, neglect, and alcoholism. In addition, the practice of Native Spirituality in my home made my life a living hell as a child. Eerie things happened constantly—mystical experiences that were far more than just feelings but were strange and frightening realities. Far too many of these occurred to discount them as imagination or coincidence. For instance, when my parents left us at home alone at night, some presence would almost always harass us, as though watching us through the windows. We'd all race to the other side of the house, screaming and crying in terror. Only after the visitation ended would we slowly come out of hiding.

We used to camp out on our lawn in canvas tents for fun. But when darkness began to blanket the daylight, we would see a mystical light appear across the river as though someone was carrying a torch—only no one visible. Not so long ago, this same mystical light appeared in another area of the same community. And in times past, we also would hear a baby crying when there was no baby present. Even if our neighbors had had a baby, they lived too far away for us to hear it cry.

I also saw silhouettes of people, and a big black dog appeared inside our home at night a few times and then disappeared. But we didn't own a big black dog. Once when this happened, the next morning I told Dad, "There was a big black dog running around inside the house last night. He ran from your room to our bedroom looking at everyone. I was sleeping on the couch so I had a better view of where he came from and where he went. Then suddenly, he went through the door and was gone."

"Someone shapeshifting," Dad told me. "Checking us out to see what was going on in our home." Native Spirituality believes that shapeshifting allows one to take on an animal form while visiting on the astral plane. The enemy loves to cripple and control people through fear. Nightmares were also a part of this evil package. Sometimes, I'd wake up to find a creature like a lizard crawling on my legs over the top of the blankets. Something told me to pinch it as hard as I could on its feet. When I did, it disappeared. A few times I awoke to find about the first three inches of the top edge of the blanket so heavy that I had to fight and struggle to get it off. Yet, there was nothing on it, and because I was not under the covering of the shed blood of the Lord Jesus Christ, I would stay awake for hours, terrified about returning to sleep, fearing that whatever it was would return. Now that I am a born-again Christian I rarely have nightmares, but when I do, I rebuke the enemy in Jesus' name. It flees, and I fall right back to sleep. That's the power in Jesus' name.

Despite the strain and stresses of home life, there were times that life on our farm in a ranch-style house on the prairies was fun. My siblings and I loved to race to the creek downhill from our house, away from where our horses, cows, pigs, geese, and chickens would be. One day while my parents were in town shopping, my brother decided we should have a rodeo at the barn. We all ran to get the horses ready. We selected a two-year-old stud that wasn't broken in yet to compete against each other. He was a wild one, and most of us got bucked off immediately. Only one brother could stay on for a couple of minutes. We soon got tired of the horses, so we would move on to riding the pigs. No one was able to stay on the pigs longer than the horse—except our second eldest brother who stayed on for a minute. I suppose this is what happens when there's no television to watch, but we were never bored and always found something to do.

But in spite of these "normal" childhood experiences, an underlying current of a mystical spirituality permeated our young lives. In fact, it affected nearly every aspect of our lives. One day a Métis Settlement counselor came to our door to warn us about our river water. "You've got mercury being dumped into the water from upstream, and if you ingest too much of it, it could be harmful." Most people had water wells, but too often, they were rusty because the metal mechanisms didn't dry. Our well water tasted like rust and was so horrible we just didn't want to drink it. When Papa asked what we should do, I suggested using swamp water, which was very cold and clean.

"Let me show you something," he said to me one day. He got out some metal rods used for water dowsing, and we began to walk along slowly.

"See how the rods are swinging back and forth," he said. "This tells us there is water in that exact spot underground." We then began laughing to ourselves, happy to have found water nearby. In our ignorance at the time, we didn't know where this power was coming from or that we were practicing witchcraft. In full confidence, Dad started to dig until he reached the water, and that is where we installed the well.

PAPA'S LIFE AND TIMES

Papa Joe was a blue-eyed, short, stocky man who smoked and drank heavily but was a hardworking man nonetheless. If he was out of work, he was quite resourceful and successful in winning contracts for logging or house building. He was a twin born in March 1929 into a family of sixteen children. Times were really tough in the hungry thirties. My great-grandmother, Eliza, raised Papa due to his mother's hardship raising his twin and his older siblings and trying to keep up with housework at the same time. Papa went to school in another community and would constantly run away until the school got tired of looking for him. He finally returned to Great-Grandma's care and never went back to school.

During this time, Great-Grandma Eliza did her best to teach Papa survival skills. She took him on berry picking trips and then canned the berries for the cold winter months. Papa shared a story with me one day about a trip picking chokecherries. Great-Grandma was short and always wore long skirts. When they reached the picking area, she told Papa, "Climb that chokecherry tree and bring me down a branch." Papa decided he'd play a prank and let go of the branch, and when he did, the branch sprang back upwards, grabbing Great-Grandma and her pail of berries. "You're going to pay for this!" she screamed. Papa ran away to his biological parents, which he often did when he got into trouble. Then, when Great-Grandma settled down, she brought him back.

When Papa got a little older, Great-Grandma told him about the Frog Lake Massacre, which took place on April 2, 1885, when she was only thirteen years old. The massacre, which occurred during 1884 and 1885, was part of a larger resistance, known as the North-west Resistance, among the Cree and Métis in the Saskatchewan District. The Frog Lake Massacre was one of the most influential events of the Northwest Resistance. It ended in open-armed rebellion against the Dominion government of the Northwest Territories. The following account describes what happened:

> Incited by hunger and mistreatment rather than political motives, a breakaway element of the Plains Cree murdered nine White men on the morning of April 2, 1885, in Frog Lake (now Alberta), North-West Territories. Big Bear, chief of the Plains Cree in the

> region, sought improved conditions for Treaty Indians through peaceful means and unity among the tribes. However, the food shortage that followed the virtual extinction of the buffalo left his people near starvation and weakened his authority. Disaffection focused upon Thomas Quinn, an Indian agent who treated the Cree with harshness and arrogance. Before dawn on April 2, a party of warriors captured Quinn at his home. The Cree, led by war chief Wandering Spirit (KaPapamahchakwew) and Ayimâsis, Big Bear's son, took more prisoners as they occupied the village. Shortly before 11 a.m., the prisoners were ordered to move to an encampment about 2 km from Frog Lake.[1]

"It was a terrifying time for everyone," Great-Grandma Eliza said, "whether they were directly or indirectly involved." Papa's young eyes stared widely at his great-grandmother as she continued her story. "Two priests and seven others lost their lives."

Eliza often told Papa how their group chose her to run through the forest late at night to the priest's house so their enemies wouldn't spot her. She'd return early in the morning with bags of food, happy to have arrived safe and sound. She talked about the kidnapping of a couple of Caucasian women immediately after the rebellion, but she said that, even though it was a risky undertaking, it was for their own protection from people of their own tribe. They were eventually released unharmed when all danger was gone. Eliza talked about the extensive looting afterwards as well. These vivid memories of terror remained etched in her head until she passed away at the age of 102. And she passed the details and memory onto Papa.

Great-Grandma told Papa of other rebellions that were happening simultaneously, such as the second Riel Rebellion in 1885.

This story begins in 1884, when the Métis on the Saskatchewan River sent a delegation to Louis Riel, who was teaching school in Montana. The delegation asked him to come up and help them, and Mr. Riel accepted their invitation. For a time, he devoted himself to attempting to obtain the redress of the Metis' grievances by constitutional means, but gradually became more erratic and extreme. In the spring, he set up a provisional government at Batoche, on the South Saskatchewan River. A detachment of Northwest Mounted Police, sent to nip the rebellion in the bud, were defeated by the Métis under Gabriel Dumont—and the fat was in the fire. For a time, there was danger of an Indian uprising, and the Indians under Big Bear actually massacred most of the Whites at the Hudson's Bay Company post of Frog Lake. The Northwest Mounted Police were forced to abandon first Fort Carlton and later Fort Pitt; and the Whites in the Saskatchewan Valley were forced to take refuge within the stockades at Battleford.

We often heard stories about the troubling times and the suffering, distress, and murder the First Nations people experienced.

We often heard stories like these from our grandparents and great-great grandmother about the troubling times and the suffering, distress, and murder the First Nations people experienced prior to and during the Riel Rebellion. Papa frequently shared how Grandpa's two elder brothers fled from the Riel Rebellion to British Columbia, and how another fled to the United States. Yet, another brother had joined the military but died in France and was buried there.

Grandpa repeatedly shared how we are legally Treaty Indians because we did not sell our treaty rights that guarantees bands a tract of land, medical services, aid in times of famine or hardship, farming tools, training, livestock, the right to hunt and fish, and protection in exchange for the extinguishment of our title to the land to the Canadian government by signing the Métis Scrip certificates. He stated that our forefathers were Treaty Indians and Chiefs of Indian Reserves who fought for the retention of our treaties and signed the treaties with the Government of Canada. Others chose to surrender their rights due to economic hardship. Métis Scrip certificates could be redeemed for cash, or for land of equivalent value. Yet, today our family is considered to be Métis even though we surrendered nothing.

Our forefathers and First Nations people up to the present always have had some sort of ceremony, either with sweet grass, a sweat, or a pipe, prior to receiving Treaty payments or before entering into negotiations for land claims. In essence, they thank the "Great Spirit" in these ceremonies. (This is not the Holy Spirit of the Bible, which I will talk about later in the book.) These practices are so wrong. Is it any wonder that First Nations communities are rife with nepotism in chief and council? The ceremonies are actually a form of witchcraft (or shamanism), which is disobedience and rebellion against the true God. Unless repentance and turning to Christ take place, God will not remove their bondages and oppression nor bless and heal these people.

Just prior to the Riel Rebellion, Gabriel Dumont gave my great-great-grandfather the task of recruiting rebels for Louis Riel's cause. For that, my great-great-grandfather was arrested, prosecuted, and found guilty. He was subsequently sentenced to seven years in prison at the Stony Mountain Penitentiary. However, some believe that he was released approximately nine months later. Though he was Métis, he too was one of the chiefs that signed the Treaty. His younger brother later succeeded him, due to the fact that the Government of Canada no longer recognized him as chief because of his involvement in the Riel Rebellion. It was his punishment.

In the late 1940s, a few years after Mama came out of the residential schools, she and Papa met at a rodeo in northern Alberta where Papa was competing in amateur bareback competitions. They fell in love and subsequently got married at a church in Mama's community. During the course of their marriage, Mama bore sixteen children—ten daughters and six sons.

Papa worked long hard hours to put food on the table and

clothes on us. Often, he was gone for weeks logging in different geographical areas, such as B.C. and parts of Alberta. He eventually moved his family to northern Alberta where he started his own logging company, which he successfully ran for a few years prior to caring for his parents.

With such a big family to care for, Papa frequently went hunting or fur trapping with his team of twin horses—one male and one female. He gave me the female and allowed me to name them both. I chose the names King and Queen. He always took tobacco along to leave at the kill site to give thanks to the creator and to thank the animal for its sacrifice of life to sustain us.

One sunny autumn day, he hitched up our horses to a wagon with hunting supplies and camping gear. He was gone a couple of days, and I was looking forward to seeing him come home with our horses. But the Sunday he arrived, I saw a sight that broke my heart. From a distance, I could tell Papa was riding a horse that I knew wasn't my Queen!

When Papa reached the house, I stood there crying. "She is dead, isn't she?" I asked through my sobs. I already knew what the answer would be.

"Yes," he said, "I'm sorry—I'll get you another horse." He then told me how he had tied Queen to a tree, and when she smelled a moose, it spooked her, and she choked herself to death trying to get away.

Upon hearing the story of Queen's death, I wept bitterly. She was the gentlest, smartest horse I'd ever known, and I loved her dearly. We used to crawl in and around her legs and she wouldn't move until we were done playing. One incident stands out in my mind. One of my sisters, who was born with polio, begged me to take her for a horse ride. I told her I'd ask Mom. Mom didn't agree at first until I assured her I would only walk the horse. So, off we went up a hill. We were halfway up when suddenly Queen came to a dead stop. I hit her gently on her side to encourage her to move forward, but she wouldn't move. I then turned around to see what was going on. Unbeknownst to me, my physically handicapped sister had slid halfway down one side. Only when I had pulled her back up would Queen continue. She was such a precious and loyal horse.

Papa eventually bought me another horse, one that looked exactly like Black Beauty—and that's what I named her. Although she could never replace Queen, she had her own distinct qualities. She was a beauty—muscular and very powerful too—and won a lot of races. Many people asked Papa if they could buy her, but he'd always tell them to ask me. And of course, the reply was always no.

When another hunting trip came along, I went with Papa. He allowed me to go because it was just for one day. The trek was hard as we had to wade through a slough. Papa took his moose caller with him, and when one answered the call, he carefully aimed and killed it. Before he started to skin it though, he told me we had to leave tobacco to give thanks for everything (such as meat for food and hide for drums and clothing). He then proceeded to a nearby tree, left tobacco at the base, and returned to skin the moose. We took what we could lug home. Papa would return later with help to fetch the rest.

When drums made from animal hides are used to worship any god(s) and then reused by that person to worship the True God, that is an abomination because God will not share in the worship of idols or demons. It is also idolatrous when a hunter that kills an animal thinks it gave up its life for some physical use, such as food or hide, and then the hunter leaves a thank offering of tobacco. Many Native arts and crafts are created using hides from animals that were offered up to the gods of this world. Native arts and jewelry with certain symbols representing darkness are another example of ungodly worship. For instance, sometimes the uncut loops of rugs are supposed to trap evil. This approach is similar to using dream catchers or any artwork that symbolizes graven images. Carving spirit guides on totem poles does not bring glory, honor, or exaltation to the Lord God, our Creator, in any way. Always pray before purchasing Native art, as in most cases, pagan practitioners pray occultic prayers (that is, do incantations) over such items to move people to buy them—even unnecessarily—in order to increase sales. Continued purchases and possession of such items could eventually have one in bondage to spending money foolishly and unnecessarily to feed the flesh. The enemy does not care whether or not we have basic necessities such as food and clothing—all he cares about is promoting his lies in order to capture more unsuspecting souls and leading people further toward eternal destruction.

PAPA APPRENTICES AS MEDICINE MAN

> Beware lest any man spoil you through philosophy and vain deceit, after the tradition of men, after the rudiments of the world, and not after Christ. (Colossians 2:8)

Late in Grandpa John's life, he chose my papa to take over his practices as medicine man for he knew his time on earth was drawing to an end. "It's time to pass down to you," he told my papa, "the artifacts and my knowledge of the spirit world." He had been involved with this spirituality for decades, believing it to be the path to the true God. Papa began accompanying Grandpa John in order to learn to perform pipe ceremonies or sweat lodge ceremonies wherever they were invited to do them. Papa never did express his feelings about his indoctrination to Native Spirituality. When people are chosen to carry on these teachings, most don't question it; rather, they accept it as fulfilling an obligation. I'm quite certain Papa may have just accepted it as an act of obedience and duty.

Grandpa John never permitted females to participate in his sweat lodge ceremonies nor allowed a menstruating female to enter his home. That was the most embarrassing question ever, and a few times I purposely said "no" when asked. It is said that a woman is the most powerful during menstruation. Apparently, the powers of the medicine man are lost if a woman is in her "moon-time." One other thing Grandpa taught us is to never commit suicide. Contrary to what some are teaching about Native Spirituality, suicide was never part of any teaching I heard. If it were so, our aboriginal population in Canada would not number just over one million, the highest stats ever in history (with 4.5 million in the U.S.).

One very bitter cold January day, most of us kids were ill with a horrible flu bug, and my sister and I lay sick in bed. The room was spinning wildly around me, and I thought I would die. Keeping my eyes shut helped diminish some of the spinning and the nausea. Mama came to check on us and told us that Papa had gone to get Grandpa to come and heal us because we were so sick.

When Grandpa finally arrived, he brewed up some kind of bitter concoction for us to drink. First, he gave it to my sister, then it was my turn. I really wanted him to leave me alone as I didn't want to move an inch. The concoction he gave us didn't work because it was about another week before we finally felt well enough to move about. Grandpa came over at other times to try and heal us when we were sick, but I don't ever recall it working. I felt sure it was just a waste of time. Another man used to try to heal us, and he'd say, "You've got to have faith in me!" We always joked about that, although not in his presence.

Grandpa John left his estate to Papa, but Papa's siblings felt rejected when there was nothing for them. So Papa told them to go to the house and take whatever they wanted. Uncle Bert took the pipe that Grandpa John handed down to Papa to use in his practices as medicine man and kept it in his possession for years. It finally burned up in his sweat lodge after he threatened to stop our Christian funeral services for a family member. He didn't know Who he was dealing with—the one and only true Almighty God. How I wish my siblings and I had been introduced to Him when we were young. How much different our lives would have been had that happened, for both my parents and us kids.

Mama

Mama was a gentle, soft-spoken, kind, and loving lady. She was very pretty and tall, and she had black hair and brown eyes. She was always concerned for our health and well-being. She had a special place for us in her heart, and it was very unfortunate that she passed on at an early age. It was a devastating blow, for she was the glue of love that bonded our family. I thank the Lord that her legacy lived on in each of us for, after mourning her passing, we stayed glued together, in spite of being sick with grief for the first couple of years.

Mama was a residential school survivor, but she never mentioned the school she attended. Many aboriginal children did not mention these schools, nor did they discuss what happened in their formative years. It was not until some residential school survivors stepped forward and broke the code of silence that we began to hear of the atrocities suffered at the hands of their schoolteachers, often priests and nuns. The majority of children in the Canadian residential schools and the U.S. boarding schools suffered abuse, either physical, emotional, sexual or all three. The effects of such abuse were far-reaching and lasting:

> The unresolved trauma of Aboriginal people who experienced or witnessed physical or sexual abuse in the residential school system is passed on from generation to generation. The ongoing cycle of intergenerational abuse in Aboriginal communities is the legacy of physical and sexual abuse in residential schools.[2]

Nevertheless, although Mama had her own scars to bear from her childhood, she was a loving and devoted mother to her children.

Mama had her hands full ever since I can remember, with so many children to nurture, so much cooking and cleaning, and getting school-aged children ready for school. There were two big gardens to look after in the summer and tons of canning to do in the fall. I helped Mama with household chores or looked after my baby brother who thought I was his mama. One day, he got sick, and I pleaded with Mama to get him to a doctor because his legs were swelling. The doctor gave Mama a prescription for him, and the swelling went down in a few days.

Portrait of Native students at St. Paul's Indian Industrial School, Middlechurch, Manitoba, 1901

Aboriginal children in class at the Roman Catholic-run Fort George Catholic Indian Residential School, Fort George, Quebec, 1939

Aboriginal students and staff assembled outside the Kamloops Indian Residential School, Kamloops, British Columbia, 1934 Archives Deschâtelets.

I volunteered to wash the baby diapers while Mama was either cooking or cleaning. In the summertime, I helped seed the gardens, and also weed and water them. And while everyone else was out playing and just being able to enjoy their youth, I was mostly stuck indoors helping. So when Mama passed on, I already knew what had to be done. My own childhood ceased to exist when she died, because I had to become a mother overnight to eight younger siblings. Those were very difficult times indeed, and some of us succumbed to anger and bitterness, which became bondages, as we, not dealing with these sins, carried them into our adult lives. Only when we repented did we find release from these prisons of sin through the Lord Jesus Christ. I thank God that while we may have lost Mom, He kept us together under circumstances that cause most families to fall apart and separate.

After Mama's passing, Papa continued working until his parents could no longer care for themselves, but he waited until we were all grown up and could fend for ourselves before he left to care for his ailing and aging parents.

I still remember very clearly the day he told me he was leaving. I had just come home from shopping, and Papa was hanging up the telephone after speaking with his mom. He turned to me with a sober look on his face and said, "Nanci, I just spoke to your Grandma. She and Grandpa want me to come up and care for them now that you kids are grown. They are getting along in years and need help. Since I am their only child with grown children, they felt it best to ask me to move in with them." Of course, I was saddened and concerned by this move, but at the same time, it put me in a position to think about my life in a more serious manner.

"Well, you have obviously made your decision to relocate," I sadly replied, "and if that is what you feel you must do, then I can't stop you from leaving us." Papa told me he would not leave until the house was sold. About a month later, it did sell, and thus, he packed up and was gone.

✠✠✠✠✠✠✠✠✠✠✠

While growing up, I spent a lot of time with my paternal grandparents, and I was very inquisitive about our family history. I loved listening to them talk about such things as birth places and residences, tell stories of the past fur trade, their travels, the Riel Rebellion, and the Frog Lake Massacre, and how a lot of children and adults didn't survive illnesses.

It always amazed me how my ancestors traveled great distances by foot, dog sleds, Red River carts, horses, or canoes and endured great hardships prior to the existence of planes, trains, and automobiles. They were often forced to contend with epidemics like the flu, small pox, and measles, which left hundreds of fatalities in their wake; and sub-arctic blizzards froze many people and animals to death.

My ancestors survived by hunting, trapping, and working as interpreters or guides for the Hudson's Bay Company and the North West Company. Employment needs took them crisscrossing Upper and Lower Canada and over to Western Canada, to such areas as Lesser Slave Lake, Athabasca Landing, and Peace River.

After learning all this, I thought, *it's no wonder Papa chose to hunt for sustenance and trap animals for the fur trade, and why later he started his own logging company.* When he injured his leg in a logging accident, he was hospitalized for quite some time. Oh, how he hated being in the hospital with his leg straddled in an elevated position, but he was also worried about us, his children. I went to visit him as often as I could during our school lunch break as the school was just across from the hospital.

Not all our family members or ancestors chose to engage in the fur trade; others chose agriculture or the military as their professions. Sometime after Papa's logging accident, he decided to get involved in agriculture and began farming our fields and selling the crops. I often helped him bale when he was working the fields. A few decades later, when I landed a position with the justice system and began my tenure as a Correctional Officer in the provincial system, I often marveled at why I was seemingly the only descendant who chose to do that. Then, for the first time, I began meeting other relatives in the same profession. I wondered too, what had happened to my French relatives; then I met a couple of them when I was employed with Corrections. One is also a Correctional Officer and the other is a floor-layer whom I hired to do my floors. When we began talking about our backgrounds, we realized right away that we were related as we had both extensively traced our genealogies.

As I look back and reflect upon the major events and themes of my life, in the light of Scripture and contemporary spiritual movements, I see my situation and experiences weren't unique. Countless other people—not only Native Americans—are traveling through this terrible veil of tears and darkness with spiritual blindness. They are believing the lie that all religions are one and denying the glorious saving Gospel. There is no escaping the truth: all non-Christian religions deny the Gospel in one way or another. If they offer any kind of "salvation" for man, it is always a plan where man must earn his way, and sin is never dealt with.

Two

RELIGIOUS INFLUENCES

> Then said Jesus unto them again, Verily, verily, I say unto you, I am the door of the sheep. All that ever came before me are thieves and robbers: but the sheep did not hear them. I am the door: by me if any man enter in, he shall be saved, and shall go in and out, and find pasture. The thief cometh not, but for to steal, and to kill, and to destroy: I am come that they might have life, and that they might have it more abundantly. (John 10-7-10)

OUR CATHOLIC INFLUENCE

Growing up in a syncretistic environment left me vulnerable to deception in many different ways. For example, I never questioned whether I would make it to Heaven upon death. I took it for granted that as long as I was baptized as a baby, confessed my sins to the priest, did penance, and was good, I would make it to Heaven. These were some of the things I learned from the Roman Catholic Church—and believed. But listen to what Jesus says in the Gospel of John:

> Except a man be born of water and of the Spirit, he cannot enter into the kingdom of God. That which is born of the flesh is flesh; and that which is born of the Spirit is spirit. Marvel not that I said unto thee, Ye must be born again. (John 3:5-7)

We frequently attended mass at a Roman Catholic Church on Sundays. We also attended midnight mass on Christmas Eve and special days like Easter. At church, I sometimes led in the singing, even with adults present. This made me feel special because I was the only child leading.

The priest was adamant that we do penance for our sins in order to get to Heaven and do good works. Often, they used incense at the service, and the smell of the smoke would make me sick. I got the same effect with the smells of sweet grass, sage, and fungus—all items used to worship the god of this world. We do not have God-given authority to smudge ourselves as a means of purification. Only the Lord Jesus Christ can purify us from our sins. Only He has that authority as He died on the Cross to redeem those who are willing to be saved from sin and eternal death. Salvation is not found in any other man, religion, or technique.

We were required to eat a wafer during communion (also called the Eucharist). The Bible calls for the celebration of the Lord's Supper as a remembrance of His sacrificial death, but the Roman Catholic approach is totally different from what the Bible says. Roman Catholicism teaches that the sacrament is to be worshiped as God and that the ceremony performed by a priest magically transforms the wafer into the very body of Jesus Christ. This is called transubstantiation, which continually re-sacrifices Jesus Christ on the altar. I praise God that the Bible says Jesus died "once for all" (Hebrews 10:10) and the act of re-sacrificing again and again does not take away sin (Hebrews 10:11). In addition, they were teaching me (and the other Native Americans) salvation by works, not by faith, which fit very well with Native Spirituality and its own variety of salvation by works.

Sometimes we had to kneel at the Stations of the Cross during Easter or go on the Lake St. Anne Pilgrimage where we would pray using the rosary. We were given votive candles for use at home. I loved going to church to hear about Jesus, but, as I mention in another part of this book, I discovered later on in life that this Catholic "Jesus" who was presented to us was portrayed much differently than the Jesus Christ in the Bible whom Paul clearly explains saves us by the grace of God, and not of our own works at all (Ephesians 2:8-9. Confession of sins to the priest played a major role in our Catholic practices. I recall one Sunday when the priest said that it would be good for me to do confession, and so we went to our separate booths. I couldn't think of anything to say, so just to appease him I confessed that I stole bread.

Growing up, I had to wear a cross that was blessed and purchased at Lake St. Anne. It had a tiny picture of Mary holding baby Jesus, and I had to learn to pray using the rosary. Contrary to the Bible's teaching, these prayers are repetitive (see Matthew 6:7) and directed at a person other than Jesus Christ, who is the only mediator between God and man (1 Timothy 2:5). Most homes had a picture of a Jesus hanging on their walls. They were lovely pictures, but I doubt Jesus Christ was fair skinned and blue eyed, seeing as He was Jewish, and I'm sure He did not look anything like those pictures. So, they worshiped a different Jesus—definitely not the same Jesus Christ who hung on the Cross at Calvary as a one-time offering for the sins of all mankind.

LAKE ST. ANNE PILGRIMAGE

Every year, my parents attended the Lake St. Anne Pilgrimage without us for a week at a time. The first pilgrimage took place in 1889, and it continues to this day and attracts many Native people from all over. Although the pilgrimage lasted only a couple of days, the travel time involved was long. Mom and Papa would attend mass several times a day, renew their Catholic faith, and pray at each Station of the Cross. There are rumors that people received healing in the lake. Lake St. Anne was previously known as Manitou Sagaikan when Native people wintered there before the buffalo disappeared, and most of the people moved away. Around 1887, a priest named Lestanc had a vision that God wanted him to keep the mission open. He was to build a shrine in honor of St. Anne, whom they claim is the grandmother of

Jesus. However, there is no St. Anne mentioned in Scripture, so this is Catholic rhetoric.

During that week when we were home alone, it was free reign. We could have made a "Home Alone" movie for all our mischief. We'd hitch up Papa's horses to our neighbor's Bennett,* gather up all the kids and the neighbor's kids, and cut loose on a wild wagon ride. We'd get the horses going full speed until someone would fall off the Bennett; we'd then stop and go full speed again. This occurred numerous times until we got caught. The Bennett belonged to a lady farmer named Lydia. She was a very hard-working individual who had farmed all of her life until retirement. Lydia was a kind and caring lady, who remains fondly etched in my memory to this day.

During that week alone, I did the laundry. By the time all the clothes were washed and I took them out to the clothesline, they were all gray because I hadn't separated them. When Mama returned from the pilgrimage and saw gray clothes, all she could do was laugh.

When I grew up, I went on a couple of Lake St. Anne Pilgrimages as a spectator. I ran into relatives and friends who were only there to party, so I joined right in since I was not interested in the services. It was one big party, and though we got lectured about it, it didn't stop us from picking up where we left off the night before. I attended a few more times only to party but finally stopped attending, except to visit people during the day and return to the city at night. Years before I became a born-again believer, I stopped attending altogether for lack of interest. It was almost as though the Lord Himself led me out of there before I even knew Him, along with other places like it. I am quite sure there were numerous divine interventions in my life prior to becoming a born-again believer. In hindsight, I can see that God was leading me straight to Himself and to His Son Jesus Christ Who is now my Lord and Savior.

---

*A Bennett is a buggy drawn by horses.

SÉANCES AND SORCERY

During my early teens in junior high school, my friends and I sometimes skipped school and had séances at a friend's home. After darkening the room, we'd sit around a table with a Ouija board in the middle of it and try to talk to the spirits of our departed loved ones. Each of us would place one or two fingers on the planchette in the middle of the board and ask the spirits questions. At the time, we had no idea we were actually practicing necromancy or that these "spirits" were demons. Although nothing really happened on the first couple of tries, it was eerie waiting to hear voices in complete darkness. Then the third time we tried, most of us girls heard a voice speaking. We all began screaming and raced to throw open the curtains to allow light into the room. That was the last time we did such a thing. The very nature of the occult environment should tell us that this is not from God, but when we are non-believers we are blinded to the truth.

> But if our gospel be hid, it is hid to them that are lost: In whom the god of this world hath blinded the minds of them which believe not, lest the light of the glorious gospel of Christ, who is the image of God, should shine unto them. For we preach not ourselves, but Christ Jesus the Lord; and ourselves your servants for Jesus' sake. For God, who commanded the light to shine out of darkness, hath shined in our hearts, to [give] the light of the knowledge of the glory of God in the face of Jesus Christ. (2 Corinthians 4:3–6)

The "politically-correct" church doctrine of our time—the veil of blindness—is that all religions are really one and basically teach the same thing. I experienced this growing up with an ungodly mixture of shamanism and other occult elements combined with Roman Catholicism. Modern Roman Catholicism in America is becoming increasingly syncretistic, as are a lot of liberal Protestant churches. (One vivid example is how some evangelical churches are now teaching yoga.)

On the other hand, Native American Spirituality shares a common foundation with paganism worldwide.

One day, after I had found the Lord, my eldest brother, Ted, told me he had not been feeling well and was planning on going to a sweat lodge for healing.

"Going to the sweat lodge will not bring you lasting healing," I blurted out. "It is the work of demons, and you will go to Hell if you do not repent. You will not find Native Spirituality taught anywhere in the Bible!"

"Nanci, you shouldn't say that!" he retorted.

"Ted, I would not say that if it weren't the truth. I love you, and that is why I tell you this. I don't want you to go to Hell. Jesus said in John 3:3 that we must be born-again to enter the kingdom of God."

"I hate it when people try to force their religion onto others!" he shot back.

I could tell I wasn't getting anywhere with him. "Ted, it is not about religion, but righteousness in Him, and I am not trying to force anything onto you—I am warning you. Besides, what do you call being baptized as a baby into the Catholic religion? Who made the decision for you to be Catholic? That is force, if you ask me." But Ted would not listen, and I felt tremendous sadness for my brother at his spiritual blindness.

All heretical teachings and evil doings stem from the worship of the god of this world. All non-Christian religions are rooted within the fallen kingdom of this world. The Bible shows a clear distinction between the kingdom of this world and the kingdom of God:

> Now the works of the flesh are manifest, which are these; Adultery, fornication, uncleanness, lasciviousness, Idolatry, witchcraft, hatred, variance, emulations, wrath, strife, seditions, heresies, Envyings, murders, drunkenness, revellings, and such like: of the which I tell you before, as I have also told you in time past, that they which do such things shall not inherit the kingdom of God. (Galatians 5:19–21)

Several passages in the book of Revelation condemn sorcery in the strongest language: 9:21; 18:23; 21:8, and 22:15. In the New Testament, several Greek words that are translated as "witchcraft" and "sorcery" stem from the root words *pharmakeus* and *pharmakeia*. This is where we get the words pharmacy and pharmaceuticals meaning drugs, potions, and poisons. *Strong's Concordance* lists these Bible usages for the words: 1) the use or the administering of drugs; 2) poisoning; 3) sorcery, magical arts, often found in connection with idolatry and fostered by it; and 4) metaph. the deceptions and seductions of idolatry.[1]

Those who are familiar with sorcery practiced by occultists know that psychoactive drugs are one of the best means shamans and sorcerers use to induce altered states of consciousness in order to attain supernatural knowledge or spirit contact. Other means include the use of drumming, chanting, and singing. All these were a big part of my "spiritual" upbringing. And they had a profoundly negative influence in my life for years to come.

A Night That Changed My Life

It's the kind of night you never wish to have—when you hear words that are too awful to comprehend. One night, when I was twenty-one, I was attending a powwow with my older sister Maggie, her husband Joe, and Marie, my brother Raymond's wife. Joe had just asked me for the time, to which I told him five minutes before eight. Five minutes later he asked me again, and my watch read the same time. That time my watch read will be implanted in my mind forever, for just as I was checking to see if perhaps my watch battery had died, a cousin, who'd been searching through the powwow for us, was suddenly standing in front us with a very strange look on his face. He then told us our brother Raymond had just been murdered.

Raymond had been out drinking, and a jealous friend decided to take advantage of Raymond when he was too drunk to defend himself. Raymond had been known for his prowess with his fists and feet during a battle. Many men had challenged him to fights because they had heard that the courts declared his limbs to be dangerous weapons. I'm not sure why they felt it was necessary to fight him, but he was always prepared to defend himself until that dreadful night when Tom, his "best friend," stabbed him twice in the heart and once in the neck. Raymond died instantly in the presence of Jane (a friend of his) and my sister May.

When our brother Will and sister Lee arrived on the scene shortly after Raymond died, there was pandemonium as Jane and my sister were screaming hysterically, "He's dead! Raymond is dead!" My brother Will raced around in a frenzy searching for the now-murderer Tom. But Tom had already been arrested, and the house had already been cordoned off, and no one was allowed to see Raymond.

Marie, Raymond's wife, took his death very hard. They had a one and half year old son of whom Raymond had been so proud. "I'm gonna make sure Dezi receives a good education and goes to college," Raymond would often say. But little Dezi would grow up, never knowing his father and the dreams he had for his son. After that night, our family tried to talk about Raymond's death whenever we could to help each other through the grieving process that would take a long time to go through. But one never really gets over the tragic loss of a family member. It is such a shock to the system.

After the death of my brother, I began to do some serious soul-searching. As I looked around my community, I found that the negative far outweighed the positive. Full-time jobs were scarce, and there were no careers that even interested me; nor would I have secured one of these positions if there were, because nepotism reigned rather than fairness. A drag-me-down system existed where members of the community would try and drag down someone who succeeded in life. Most of us would only find temporary jobs. This became my biggest motivating factor as far as setting long-term goals. I decided that living in this type of environment was not for me; it was anything but idyllic and too toxic. Thus, in 1979, I left the Métis Settlement and relocated to the city of St. Albert, where I boarded with my aunt and uncle.

+++++++++++

The religious influences in my growing up years were saturated with mysticism and occultism, both powerful elements of Native Spirituality. These influences included inducing altered states of consciousness through the use of the sacred pipe, sweats, fasts, chants, songs, dances, vision quests, dreams, and ancestor worship. Drumming, singing, and chanting, however, are the most conducive means, as they prepare one to enter into a trance more quickly. Peyote (a drug) is also a very effective way of achieving an altered state of consciousness. Some Native people who become born-again Christians end up in hyper-charismatic churches, never questioning the mystical experiences they witness or engage in. And I know of some who started off in Bible-believing churches who left, upset because they hadn't experienced anything mystical. Today's emerging "new Christianity" church is full of people seeking spiritual experiences rather than truth. So when I professed becoming a Christian, I truly believed that Christianity must be mystical as well. Years elapsed before I learned what was happening to my walk with the Lord.

The religious influences in my growing up years were saturated with mysticism and occultism, both powerful elements of Native Spirituality.

One day, the Lord Jesus Christ showed me that being born-again was not just another mystical experience, but it involved repentance (turning away from our sinful lives), faith (belief) in the Lord Jesus Christ Who is our Savior, and putting our trust in Him. The Gospel of Mark tells us, "repent ye and believe the gospel" (Mark 1:15). Too often, I had tried to *spiritualize* the Gospel, having come from a mystical background, when in reality the Gospel is a very practical way of living—incorporating a life of repentance with a daily walk of faith—trusting Jesus as Savior, Shepherd and Guide, and Provider for all of my needs.

And there was delivered unto [Jesus] the book of the prophet Esaias. And when he had opened the book, he found the place where it was written, The Spirit of the Lord is upon me, because he hath anointed me to preach the gospel to the poor; he hath sent me to heal the brokenhearted, to preach deliverance to the captives, and recovering of sight to the blind, to set at liberty them that are bruised. (Luke 4:17-18)

THREE

LIFE AND WORK "INSIDE THE WIRE"

During the mid 1980s, I began to have a deep-seated desire to work in a prison as a correctional officer. To this day, I'm not sure exactly what sparked my desire. I had driven past a particular prison in the prairies many times and often found myself thinking, "I should go to work in a prison." I procrastinated for many years before deciding to do something about this recurring idea. I was floundering hopelessly in different meaningless areas of employment and languishing in unhappy predicaments, largely due to my family troubles.

I had dropped out of high school because it was just too overwhelming to juggle schoolwork and being a child-parent to my eight younger siblings. But I comforted myself by thinking that one day I would complete my education. I always knew I should finish it because quitting just seemed so wrong. I eventually enrolled in a two-year Correctional Services Program at a community college in Alberta and graduated with a diploma in April 1992. After my graduation, I received my grade twelve diploma by passing my

GED credential. I got that diploma much later than I had ever planned, but it was important to me to have it.

Right away, I applied for a Corrections Officer position at a county jail, which, by the way, was a co-ed prison. I was hired along with five males. After completing a highly intensive week of training, we picked up our uniforms and were told to report for duty the following Monday. I was about to enter life "inside the wire."

Everything in the Canadian Provincial system is black and white when it comes to dealing with inmates. If one so much as swears at the Corrections Officers, it is an automatic fourteen-day digger time—no questions asked. (Digger is prison jargon for segregation.)

Officer Parks yelled outside cell door A207, "Inmate Slash, we are here to escort you to segregation. I want you to come out of your cell backwards with your hands behind your head until we instruct you to stop; do you understand?"

"Yes, Boss."

"R25 to R20, crack cell door A207, over!"

"R20 to R25, I copy —crack cell door A207, R20 roger out!'

"Come on out now Mr. Slash. Remember—hands behind your head—okay stop there, lower your right hand to your lower back so I can apply the handcuffs [click]—now give me your left hand [click]—now turn around and start walking forward."

"Hey Boss, the handcuffs are too tight!"

"Okay, stop so I can re-adjust them. In a couple minutes, we will arrive at the Segregation Unit. You have received fourteen days digger time for disrespecting staff, as you were informed would happen at kangaroo court. While you are there, I hope you will think about your behavior and what you can do to make some changes."

"Yes, Boss, I'm really sorry for causing trouble. I will try my best to do my time trouble free."

Approaching the Segregation Control Post, Officer Parks stated, "Officer Des Gerlaise, inmate Slash has been awarded fourteen days digger time for disrespecting staff—we will radio you to crack open his new cell."

Thus began my life as a prison guard. The first time I sent an inmate to segregation for being disrespectful, I heard the guys down the hallway stomping on the concrete floor with their steel-toed boots, each at about six feet tall plus and most of them easily weighing a good two hundred and fifty pounds, while the song, "Bad boys, bad boys, wha' cha gonna do when they come for you?" played on the radio in the background. It would have been a perfect scene from a movie, and I would have chuckled at it had it not been so serious and intense.

I was frightened the first time I walked into a prison. I have since learned that this happens a lot to new staff. First time offenders also go through a scary experience especially if they are weak because no one is there to protect them from the predators. It's almost like parents leaving on a shopping trip or on holidays and the kids are left at home alone—only to have the older siblings threatening to beat up the younger ones, except in prison the consequences are much worse.

On my first day at work, which happened to be a day shift, they sent me to a specific male unit that was allegedly the worst unit to work in. It was eerily quiet except that all the cons lined up on the second floor from one end of the unit to the other to check out this new rookie—me. They were trying to unnerve me by putting on a formidable appearance to see what I would do. Outwardly, I ignored them completely and paid attention to what my partner was teaching me about the post. Inwardly, I was acutely aware of every eye upon me. In prison, inmates will invariably test new staff or—the proper term for new staff— 'rookie.' I was waiting for the test, keeping an eye out for any unusual activities or requests from the inmates, for I knew without a doubt it was coming.

On the second day, I arrived at the unit and joined my senior partner to take our positions at our open control post. A half-hour into the shift, my partner left me alone when he went into the back office to write some overdue reports. A number of inmates worked on the early morning highway crew, so they had to get an early-bird breakfast and be at the bus on time. As the minutes ticked on, I felt something was amiss. I could plainly see that all the cons were congregating at the far end of the unit and looking at me every few seconds. Alone at the control post, I was obviously the subject of their conversation. Nevertheless, I was enthusiastically ready for them for my training kicked in at that exact moment.

Suddenly, approximately twenty inmates stood right before my open control post, trying to frighten and intimidate me. Imagine that—day two—and you're alone with the prisoners. "Hey, can I call my lawyer?" one inmate asked me. We had the controls for the telephones, radios, and televisions at our posts. The legal offices were closed when the prisoners left early in the morning and after they returned late at night. And the lawyers didn't want calls at home because so many of the calls were of a frivolous nature.

"I can't turn on the phones just yet," I called out. If allowed one, I would have to turn them on for everyone. "You can go into the back office and have my partner put the call through for you under supervision," I added. The prisoner was fine with that, so I advised my senior partner by phone and that particular inmate got his legal call.

Then another inmate propelled his skinny body toward the control post and asked the same question. I gave him the same answer, but this inmate was putting me to the test, for he started screaming and yelling at me. "The rules and regulations suck around here!"

This was the wrong response, so I jumped up and pointed at him. "Listen, if you didn't get yourself in here in the first place, you wouldn't be standing here complaining about rules and regulations. I did not come here to make up rules and regulations; I came here to enforce them!" With that, all the inmates returned to their cells. I had gained their respect and was now called "Boss." The word "Boss" is only given to Correctional Officers who have gained the inmates' respect.

A couple weeks later, inmate Slash from the Highway Crew returned from work, and upon turning in his Institutional Identification, he stood looking at me with a look that said, "I'm up to no good!" On his way back to his cell, he was stopping to speak with any inmate within hearing range as to what he was about to do. I kept this inmate constantly under surveillance and waited with baited breath. By the time he arrived at his cell, all the inmates he had spoken to along the way had congregated outside his cell. Suddenly, the cell call rang at the control post from his cell asking me nicely enough to turn up the radios.

"No, the noise level is too high in here already," I replied. With that he screamed,

"Turn them up now!"

I replied, "You be quiet, or I will shut them all off!" There was dead silence at the other end, except for the other inmates laughing at him. Once again, I had shown them who was boss. Any other outcome would have been bad news for me.

ENTER THE SWEAT LODGE

In the late 1990s, prior to becoming born-again, I entered competitions for a position as a caseworker at a Provincial community corrections center. A requirement for the competitions was a week-long sensitivity training program in Native Spirituality.

During the training, we were asked to work out a scheduling roster, for they required staff to spend time with Native elders. We were also required to participate in a sweat lodge ceremony. Our female elder, Rose, who conducted the sweat lodge ceremony for the female participants, gathered us all together and said it was time for a cleansing and healing ceremony.

Rose had already set up the lodge and was ready to go. We got into our long nightgowns, grabbed our towels, and crawled into the sweat lodge, beginning from the east and entering counterclockwise. When we were all seated, Rose entered last. "Hand me that pail of water," she instructed the doorkeeper. When she was handed the pail, she began to pour the water over the heated rocks inside the pit of the sweat lodge. Once that was done, Rose instructed the doorkeeper to close the flap. It was pitch black—there was nothing but darkness. Rose began her chanting, inviting the ancestors to enter the lodge and in prayer began asking for a cleansing and healing for all of us. The elders supposedly impart secret knowledge from the ancestors to the participants.

During the first round, Rose told us that the ancestors had entered the sweat lodge. I did not hear anything spectacular, like ancestors talking but only what sounded like a flapping of birds' wings. It was so hot inside the sweat lodge that we kept fanning ourselves with our nightgowns and were so glad when we could come out for air!

"Oh Rose! It's so hard to breathe in there with all that heat!" one woman exclaimed in a bit of a panicky tone.

"Thank goodness for breaks in between rounds!" another said, wiping the sweat from her brow.

"I'll try not to make it so hot," Rose answered, "but we have to have you girls cleansed spiritually—you know that."

Then we went back inside for a few more rounds.

During the final day of the competitions, we were asked to make a speech. When it was my turn, it was like someone was holding my jaws shut to keep me from talking. Natives believe that something like this can happen when a curse is used to keep someone from winning a competition or to keep the person from telling the truth. Someone who feels threatened by another person who has more work experience may resort to such dirty tactics to win a competition. Not being able to speak was actually a blessing in disguise though. Had I stayed, I would have slid deeper into paganism, making it harder for me to receive the Gospel. And I wouldn't have met the people God wanted me to meet in order to have *Muddy Waters* published. In this case, not winning that competition was the best thing that could have happened to me.

Inside a sweat lodge, there is a pit. When I think of that pit, I can't help thinking of when the Bible mentions the term "pit." It is almost always referring to either Hell or a place of death or danger. For example, in the Book of Psalms, it says:

> I will exalt you, O LORD, for you lifted me out of the depths and did not let my enemies gloat over me. O LORD my God, I called to you for help and you healed me. O LORD, you brought me up from the grave; you spared me from going down into the pit. (Psalm 30:1–3)

The depiction here is clear: depths, the grave, the pit, darkness, destruction, corruption, mire, and slime. This clearly shows that the pit is contrary to the Word of God, which should bring us to the understanding that we need to flee from and be delivered from the pit.

Native Spirituality Inside the Wire

Up until more recent years, incarcerated Native Americans in Canadian prisons were not allowed to engage in their religious practices nor were they given spiritual guidance from chaplains of their beliefs. Now, however, that has changed and the Canadian prisons allow the practice of Native Spirituality through hired elders who have the same standing ascribed to chaplains. They also get paid the same as regular chaplains. They work Monday through Friday and sometimes hold weekend sweat lodge or pipe ceremonies. This is often the first time most aboriginal inmates learn about Native Spirituality because many were never exposed to it or practiced it at home. Canadian prisons are mandated by law to offer religious and spiritual accommodations to any inmates who desire to continue in their faith while in custody.

Institutional chaplains make spiritual guidance readily available to staff members and inmates of all religious traditions. For example, a Roman Catholic priest is expected to avail himself to provide spiritual guidance to anyone, whether he or she is of a Christian, Muslim, or Buddhist background. Spiritual leaders from outside institutions do occasionally, however, come in to perform worship services. For example, rabbis do accept proselytes to Judaism while incarcerated, but if the inmate's mother is not of Jewish origin, the inmate is not obligated to follow the kosher diet that forbids eating shellfish and pork.

Religious diets are honored but are done in consultation with Kitchen Management according to prison protocols. If the chaplain or the institutional staff challenges the legitimacy of an inmate's request, they will confer with a leader of the religion in question. Some inmates will attempt to request a religious diet because they hate a certain food group. For example, one inmate stated that he was Jewish and could not eat fish because he said his god, Allah, (actually the Muslim god) forbids it. When questioned about his surname, it was not Jewish. In this kind of circumstance, a rabbi would need to be called in to assess this inmate's claim. Upon investigation, it will be determined if the request was indeed legitimate. In the case above, it was denied.

Some who are practicing Native Spirituality are serious about following the teachings, but others try to take advantage of it because it is the only religion that uses tobacco in its worship. General tobacco usage was banned from Canadian prisons some years ago. Since then, there has been an influx of new "worshippers" of Native Spirituality.

There was a problem with the sweat lodges in the past because inmates were allowed weekend access to conduct their own sweats. In one case, an inmate who was apprenticing to become an elder was put in charge. Things didn't go as the institutional elder expected because the inmates were using substances in the sweat lodge, and one inmate who had gone through a sex-change operation was offering sexual favors. Reports trickled in regarding these issues, and eventually the sweat lodge was closed unless an elder was present.

That didn't stop them from burning sage or smudging in their cells to mask pungent substances; nor did practicing Native Spirituality stop them from transporting drugs inside a medicine bundle in order to carry on drug dealing. Some inmates were refusing to open their bundles, claiming desecration when there was, in fact, an illegal substance inside. What they did not bank on was that I requested that a supervisor contact the elder to come in to inspect the bundle, and usually that was enough to cause the person to open his bundle.

While a large proportion of aboriginal inmates proclaim Christianity as their faith, and they practice Christian beliefs, some syncretize their Christian faith with Native Spirituality. This is a dangerous spiritual mix. A very disconcerting aspect is that anxiety and hostility can arise due to the horrendous experiences at the residential schools between the victims who practice Native Spirituality and the perpetrators who profess Christianity.

++++++++++++

The years I have been working in the Canadian prison system have allowed me some very unique opportunities to share my faith and my past experiences with both prisoners and co-workers. It has also been a daily reminder to me of just how desperately in need man is for a Savior. Whether Native, white, black, Hispanic, Jewish, or any other race, across the board, all mankind needs a Savior. And there is only One. In all the other religions, no one within those religions has offered an atonement for sin and none has risen from the dead. While I spend my days with those who are behind bars, imprisoned, without freedom to come and go as they please, the reality is that there are men and women walking the streets all through the world who are in just as much bondage as these inmates.

> Then spake Jesus again unto them, saying, I am the light of the world: he that followeth me shall not walk in darkness, but shall have the light of life. (John 8:12)

Save me, O God; for the waters are come in unto my soul. I sink in deep mire, where there is no standing: I am come into deep waters, where the floods overflow me. (Psalm 69:1–2)

Four

Light in the Midst of Darkness

A righteous man falling down before the wicked is as a troubled fountain, and a corrupt spring. (Proverbs 25:26)

When I was eight, Mama gave me a small New Testament that she had kept. Several verses stuck with me during the hard years to come. The first was John 3:16:

> For God so loved the world, that he gave his only begotten Son, that whosoever believeth in him should not perish, but have everlasting life.

I understood even then that when we reject Jesus Christ as Lord and Savior, our reward will be eternal damnation. But I didn't really understand what Christ could do for me. I thought I was too bad to be saved by Him—as if it were a matter of anything I could do in and of myself to be saved.

Some First Nations people don't understand Christianity and believe it's a white man's religion. But John 3:16 does not say "For God so loved the white man." It says "For God so loved the world."

That means everyone. Jesus Christ was a Middle Eastern Jew, not a European. In the Bible, it says that it is the Lord's will that no one should perish, but that all should come to repentance (2 Peter 3:9).

Another verse that spoke to me as a young child was Matthew 9:13:

> But go ye and learn what that meaneth, I will have mercy, and not sacrifice: for I am not come to call the righteous, but sinners to repentance.

Young as I was, I still could see the results of sin in my own family, in myself, and in other families around me. There was no peace or joy, only much fear, fighting, abuse, neglect, and drunkenness. And as I grew older, I learned about war, terrorism, and trouble in other parts of the world. I was struck by Revelation 3:20:

> Behold, I stand at the door, and knock: if any man hear my voice, and open the door, I will come in to him, and will sup with him, and he with me.

As a child, I took this literally and often used to wait for the Lord Jesus to appear at our family dinner table.

After Mom passed away, I felt like my siblings and I were discarded rags. Life got even harder as I was continually hounded by demons, and Papa drank even more than ever, often leaving us home alone for one to two weeks at a time. He had never learned to grieve properly and couldn't handle Mom's passing. It was at a time when school teachers did not believe anything students said about home life. So because Papa was gone most of the time, someone had to stay home with the younger siblings, which turned out to be me. I knew I needed to be in school to get an education, and the only way I felt I could get anyone's attention was to run away from home. I did, and three months later, I was caught and put in a juvenile detention center until a court date; and from there I was put in a foster home. The day after family court, the rest of my siblings were picked up at home and put in foster homes as well. Papa was given a choice to either quit drinking or lose us completely. He eventually quit drinking, and we all went home, but not until some of us were bounced around from one foster home to the next for one year.

At times, as I was growing up, I even considered suicide. As I grew older, I gave myself over to partying, immorality, drugs, fighting, and most of the forms of Native Spirituality I talk about in this book.

In 1994, a number of years after I had grown and left home, I got married, but inside I still felt something was missing in my life, and my heart had so much pain and agony.

All the while, deep within my desperate heart, I felt the Lord Jesus Christ calling me. But I had no idea what that meant or how He could want me. I was also tormented by the thought that if I became a Christian, my dad would die (for Satan will use whatever lies and terror tactics it takes to keep from losing his vice grip on sinners).

For years, I found myself caught up in an epic tug of war. On one side was the Lord Jesus Christ, and on the other side was Satan. It was spiritual chaos! No one could help me or even understand what was happening. All I could do was cry out to the Lord from the depths of my soul and ask Him to rescue me.

One day in 1998, He did.

When I heard about the prayer ministry in a local church, I scheduled myself for a ministry session. The women who ran it prayed and fasted for me for one week prior to our meeting, which ended up lasting nine hours thoroughly covering every area of sin and demonic deception and assault in my life.

That day, I knew beyond a doubt, that the Lord Jesus Christ was my Lord and Savior. I repented of and renounced all my sin, along with all my involvement in Native Spirituality. I put my trust in the death of Jesus Christ on the Cross only, where God punished Jesus, the Innocent One, for my sins that I, the guilty one, might obtain His standing as a child of God, free from recrimination or accusation.

He washed me clean of all my sin by His precious blood and broke the grip of the demonic realm over my life. He set me free from occult bondages and demonic harassment. I realized that Christianity was not the "white man's" way but God's way of salvation. Colossians 1: 12-14 made perfect sense to me:

> Giving thanks unto the Father, which hath made us

> meet to be partakers of the inheritance of the saints in light: Who hath delivered us from the power of darkness, and hath translated us into the kingdom of his dear Son: In whom we have redemption through his blood, even the forgiveness of sins.

My joy was so great that, driving home from that meeting, I had to stop at a rest area and let it overflow. I simply couldn't stop grinning. While victory from all the bondages and demonic influences didn't happen overnight, the Lord met me where I was, and He has given me the grace and strength to resist Satan's attacks. That's not to say that temptations don't come, but now I know how to recognize them and overcome them with the Holy Spirit's guidance and help. Truly, I was delivered from darkness and brought into the light.

PAPA'S ILLNESS

I was working graveyard shift one night in 1997 when the call came. My husband had returned early from his job to find a flashing telephone message. He didn't usually check those messages, only because he didn't want to awaken me during the day. But sensing something was different this time, he checked the message left by my sister, Maggie, and found it was urgent. Papa had been rushed by ambulance to the hospital in Edmonton, Alberta, and the prognosis was grim. I arose and called my boss to apprise him of what just happened and to book an impromptu annual leave. Then we sped off to Alberta, which was a twelve-hour drive. While en route, I prayed the Lord would heal Dad and raise him up from his hospital bed so he would have an opportunity to give his life and heart to the Lord and become a child of God. After two hours of pleading with God in prayer for Papa's healing, I was flooded with God's peace and felt assured that somehow Papa would be all right. The rest of the trip was peaceful and free of anxiety. Praise God!

The doctor informed us that Papa could possibly have another stroke within the first year, which could be fatal, but thankfully, that did not happen. During this time, he began to live with my brother, Max, and his wife.

In June 2007, Papa fell ill with heart, prostrate, and kidney problems and had to be hospitalized. This was the last time he was able to live on his own. It was a sad time and a difficult adjustment for him because he had lived so independently all of his life. Now he found himself at someone else's mercy.

PAPA—FROM MEDICINE MAN TO CHILD OF GOD

During the time of Papa's hospitalization for his heart problems in 2007, Pastor Fast led my dad to the Lord. He explained the Gospel of Jesus Christ to Papa so that he could understand. He explained the consequences for rejecting Jesus Christ (eternal life in Hell); and the reward for accepting Jesus Christ, which is eternal life in the kingdom of God. Once he was done, the pastor asked Papa if he would reject or accept Jesus Christ. Papa chose to accept Jesus Christ as his Lord and Savior. Heads were bowed in prayer as Papa was being led to the Lord Jesus Christ. What a blessing and a great joy to witness a parent becoming a truly born-again Christian!

On October 27, 2010, Papa had a massive heart attack, and the paramedics and doctors could not revive him. Thus, he passed on to his new eternal home with the Lord. While I was filled with a deep sadness in losing him, I knew that we would be together again someday.

After numerous family members, relatives, and friends were informed of Papa's passing, those of us who were born-again Christians came under heavy opposition from those who were into Roman Catholicism and Native Spirituality. When they became aware that a born-again Christian pastor would be conducting the services, Uncle Bert (the one who incorporated the medicine pipe into his spiritual practices) threatened to stop them. We knew he meant through sorcery, so we requested prayer from Christians worldwide. One of my brothers, Ted, who was still given to paganism, became the mouthpiece for those who opposed us. He approached my physically handicapped sister and asked her, "Can we at least hold a Catholic service?"

"I depend on the Lord for my spiritual and physical needs," she told him. "He gave me my granddaughter to raise. No, I cannot do this to Him now." Praise the Lord for her courageous stand for Him!

Another relative threatened to bring a rag to the hall where we were planning to have our Christian memorial services in order to harm us through witchcraft. But others took her home after she flipped out while walking her rag around the hall and giving everyone the "evil eye." In yet another instance, Ted's son threatened to commit suicide and ended up in the hospital with an inch deep slash on his arm. He was stitched up and discharged.

At our services, Papa's children and their respective spouses were to sit in the front row with the grandchildren in the second row. Then God intervened with His own seating arrangements—for those who were against us raced to the second row and sat down in the seats farthest left, then almost as quickly, scooted over to the far right. A few minutes later after everyone was seated, Pastor Bill began his sermon very close to where our attackers sat! They had no choice but to listen to the sermon. Throughout the services, I watched their responses. They were constantly fidgeting in their seats, under obvious conviction. I recognized their discomfort from the conviction I kept falling under when I was still lost spiritually.

Following Papa's burial, we all gathered together at the community hall for a meal. Pastor Bill said grace and then offered free CDs to anyone who requested one. As we were filling our plates, I observed an interesting interaction between my cousin and my brother Ted, who were both ahead of me in line. They were listening to a Gospel music CD that was playing.

"Whose CD is that?" I heard my cousin ask Will. "Is that the one Pastor Bill is selling? I wouldn't pay a cent for it."

Brother Ted answered, "No, it's free; you just have to ask for it."

We all went to our tables, and I saw my cousin ask Pastor Bill for a CD. I could hardly keep from laughing because the pastor's free CD was titled *Are You Ready?* by Storyteller and spoke about being ready for Judgment Day.

The day after the funeral, a prayer I had been praying for years was partially answered in a spectacular way. I had prayed with Micah 5:12 in mind on many occasions that the Lord would perform His Word as follows: "I will destroy your witchcraft and your soothsayers will be no more." I prayed this Scripture for the lives of all medicine men and women throughout North America and worldwide. Much to my joy, I learned that Uncle Bert's sweat lodge had burned to the ground with everything in it, including the pipe that had the clan-god in it. Satan's power was greatly weakened in our late grandfather's descendants that day!

Recently, a friend told me that another family member, who has since passed away, told him that my uncle had been wondering why his powers had become weak and sometimes didn't even work. Another prayer of mine had been that Uncle's followers and family would see that those powers are not from God Almighty and that they would begin questioning this pagan practice. My prayers for their salvation are yet to be fulfilled—but I am convinced they will be because our God reigns!

At another funeral—that of my late brother—Catholic services were conducted with an admixture of Native Spirituality and Christianity. I couldn't stay inside that community hall very long. I simply had to leave. Apparently, this interspiritual ecumenism, which is not at all dissimilar to what is happening in the Roman Catholic Church, is fast becoming "the norm" with regard to many professing or would-be Christians' spiritual outlook. One Catholic church in Saskatoon incorporates smudging with sweet grass while using drums and singers on special occasions—not to mention singing toward the four corners—all of which constitute pagan practices. Smudging is a purification ceremony where a designated elder uses an eagle feather to fan the smoke around each participant, supposedly to drive away evil spirits.

I am the daughter of a medicine man and the granddaughter of another one. But praise God, I am also the daughter of a medicine man-turned-believer in Jesus Christ. God was merciful and heard my prayers to save Papa, and now he too was delivered from darkness and brought into the presence of the Light of the world.

> [Jesus said] I am come a light into the world, that whosoever believeth on me should not abide in darkness. (John 12: 46)

SHARING THE GOSPEL BEHIND THE WIRE

One hot and muggy day, I reported for duty, fully expecting to be posted at my usual workstation. I walked into my boss' office only to be redeployed to the visitor control post. I was upset about it, but I had no choice in the matter. Toward the end of the day, there was a mad exodus of staff leaving for home. Then, a few minutes later, an aboriginal elder and an aboriginal parole officer came out. The elder placed his bag on the x-ray machine I was operating that was designed to scan every bag and purse entering or leaving the institution. While the x-ray machine was scanning the elder's bag, I was looking intently at the monitor to see what was in it. When it reached the other side, the elder grabbed it and left, leaving the parole officer wondering why I was looking so intently at the monitor.

"Is something wrong?" he asked.

"No," I said, "I was just looking at the elder's native regalia on the monitor." Then I turned and looked at him straight in the eyes and asked, "What if you died tonight and found yourself in Hell only because what you believed to be truth was actually lies?'"

He had a very shocked look and answered, "III ddooon't knnnoow!"

I then explained the Gospel to him and gave him a copy of an unpublished manuscript on Native Spirituality. He has since transferred three provinces away.

On another occasion, I was redeployed once again to the visitor control post. There had been a big influx of aboriginal staff coming from other institutions attending an aboriginal inmate graduation. I learned that the staff would be coming out with gifts from the inmates. Again, I found myself checking these bags. It was a rather difficult thing for me to do, seeing that the bags contained dream catchers. I prayed for the Lord's protection over me. When the last bag came through, there was clearly a manifestation taking place. The dream catcher was the largest one I'd seen that day, and when I asked the lady to open up her bag and she complied, my head reeled back hard. "Ugh!" came out of my mouth! I asked the staff member, "Don't you know these dream catchers are evil things?" She laughed. I continued by saying, "You won't be laughing on Judgment Day!" Her reply was deafening silence. I then buzzed the door, but she missed her first chance to get out. She was so unhappy about this that she took God's name in vain.

"Don't you use my God's name in vain!" I exclaimed.

Finding myself, yet again, at this fast-becoming-infamous visitor control post on another evening shift, I saw a visitor leave a hobby craft shop with what so happened to be a dream catcher. (This was a common occurrence.) I politely explained to her what it really was and how the claims of catching good dreams were actually a lie. She replied, "To each his own."

I looked at her and calmly said, "There will be no, 'To each his own' on Judgment Day!"

On yet another evening, I found myself processing inmate visitors. All was going well, and no one was alarmed on the walk-through scanner. Then a lady came in by herself excited about her son having an upcoming parole hearing.

"My son will be attending a parole hearing next week," she said, "and he'll be getting out. He's been walking on water!"

"No," I replied, "he hasn't been walking on water—there's only one Man who has walked on water, Jesus Christ, Himself!"

She said no more and remained very quiet.

I finished processing her and sent her down to the Visits and Correspondence Department for a visit with her son.

During my tenure as Correctional Officer at a Canadian

provincial jail, which also housed federal inmates, it has been my observation that most of the inmates there were incarcerated for committing crimes ranging from robbery to murder charges while under the influence of alcohol. Some of them have severed relationships with wives and children through separation or divorce and have lost other family members due to their substance abuse problems. They have also lost homes and employment, and pretty much their entire livelihood. A lot of the inmates were unable to quit abusing substances on their own. I shared my testimony with an inmate and then shared the Gospel with him prior to his release back onto the streets. I have not seen or heard from him since and hope that means he has committed his life to the Lord.

Prior to becoming a born-again believer, I was held in bondage to such things as anger, alcohol, bitterness, and unforgivingness to name a few. Where alcohol was concerned, I could not stop with only one or two alcoholic beverages. I had to keep going sometimes for days and sometimes for weeks. All these bondages fueled each other causing me to pick fights with people constantly, irrespective of whether my victims were male or female. This affected my life in many ways—such as family life, employment, relationships, etc. I would constantly take issue with the boyfriend I had at the time so I could have an excuse to go partying all weekend. I would storm away and head to the pub to get drunk—all the while thinking that I was having a good time. In my selfishness, I was only hurting myself and those closest to me. It was only by God's grace that I did not get charged with physical assault every time I got into an altercation. I was a wretched person.

I praise God that now I am set free by the grace of Jesus Christ after repenting of all these sins that had their vice-like grip on me. The chains have fallen away!

If the Son therefore shall make you free, you shall be free indeed. (John 8:36)

RECIPE FOR SPIRITUAL DISASTER

Blend a little Native Spirituality with Roman Catholicism,
Smudge it with a little sweet grass to enhance the flavor,
Dust off the monstrance and insert loose sweet grass into it.
Shake 5 minutes.
Hope you don't anger any spirits during shake up,
For you may have to appease them or go to confession.

With that confession, add a few Hail Mary's.
Next, take the golden cup and lace the inside with some sage,
Dump six crumbled wafers in the bottom of the golden cup.
Pour a little wine into the mixture—about 1/4 cup,
Mix well with talking stick and wait for spiritual disaster.

When spiritual disaster strikes,
And evil spirits are tormenting you mercilessly,
The only way out is . . . the only way to escape is . . .
Run fast to the only True God for protection and deliverance.

Do not look back; remember Lot's wife,
She looked back much to her destruction.
She turned into a pillar of salt,
'Twas her reward for disobeying God's command,
'Do not look back.'

Nanci Des Gerlaise

And no marvel; for Satan himself is transformed into an angel of light. Therefore it is no great thing if his ministers also be transformed as the ministers of righteousness; whose end shall be according to their works. (2 Corinthians 11: 14-15)

FIVE

A COUNTERFEIT VERSUS THE REAL THING

Be not carried about with divers and strange doctrines. For it is a good thing that the heart be established with grace. (Hebrews 13:9)

Many Native Americans believe that because a power lies within their spirituality or that because it is ancestral and traditional, it is right and true. But assuming that the mere presence of spiritual power means it is good can be very dangerous. The Bible is full of warnings about the subtlety and dangers of demonic powers and deception.[1]

Instead of believing that anything spiritually powerful is good, we rather must ask: What is the actual *source* of this power? Does it really connect its practitioners with a trustworthy spiritual realm? Does it originate from the one true and living God whose only Son came in the flesh and died on the Cross for our sins? Does it deliver what it promises? Or do we actually get something else? Something false and deceitful? Jesus' first reply when asked about the signs of His return was to watch out that we are not deceived. And 1 Thessalonians 5:21–22 warns us to, "Prove all things; hold fast that which is good. Abstain from all appearance of evil."

We need to test all things and see if their claims hold up in the light of truth.

TWO SOURCES OF POWER BUT ONLY ONE SOURCE OF TRUTH

Throughout the ages, an epic battle has raged between two sources of power: God's and Satan's. However, they are not in any way equal. The Eternal God created Satan and granted him limited power for a season. That battle has not ceased or desisted by any stretch of the imagination, but in our time, it has grown far more subtle, powerful, and widespread.

Second Corinthians 11:14-15 warns us that Satan is "transformed into an angel of light," and his "ministers" (demons) are "transformed as the ministers of righteousness." Thus, it is absolutely imperative that we are able to discern true from false and genuine from counterfeit.*

Why do we need discernment? some may ask. First of all, if we are Christians, born of the Holy Spirit through the atoning blood of Jesus Christ, God will judge our works and hold us accountable for decisions we make and how we live our lives.

> For other foundation can no man lay than that is laid, which is Jesus Christ. Now if any man build upon this foundation gold, silver, precious stones, wood, hay, stubble; every man's work shall be made manifest: for the day shall declare it, because it shall be revealed by fire; and the fire shall try every man's work of what sort it is. (1 Corinthians 3:11–13)

> For the time is come that judgment must begin at the house of God: and if it first begin at us, what shall the end be of them that obey not the gospel of God? (1 Peter 4:17)

On the other hand, those of you who are not born-again Christians should be very sober-minded about your eternal destination. If you do not accept His free gift of salvation and believe in Him to be your Savior and Lord, you will spend eternity in darkness where there is no good thing.

---

*See Appendix 1 for a helpful comparison chart.

> He that believeth on the Son hath everlasting life: and he that believeth not the Son shall not see life; but the wrath of God abideth on him. (John 3:36)

It's easy in this age of do-it-yourself cafeteria-style religion to become confused and to miss the truth. For instance, some professing Christians actually call Jesus Christ a shaman (a witch doctor) and the gifts of the Holy Spirit a form of shamanism or witchcraft.

This blasphemous view reveals a flagrant lack of understanding of the true character of Christ and His holiness and the true character of the devil and evil.

Still others professing to be Christians say that the works we do save us and get us into Heaven. Roman Catholicism, for instance, teaches this unbiblical doctrine (justification by works), and its influence is also widespread among Native Americans.

As a child, I used to attend a Roman Catholic Church. I loved hearing about Jesus and being chosen to help lead the hymns, but I didn't realize they were teaching me a false gospel and telling me about the wrong Jesus. The Bible says:

> For by grace are ye saved through faith; and that not of yourselves: it is the gift of God: Not of works, lest any man should boast. (Ephesians 2:8–9)

The ungodly mixture of occultism and works, as a means to obtain spiritual power, has existed for centuries among the Native peoples. Back in the 1800s and the early 1900s, the Canadian government subjected them to residential schools to "Christianize" these "pagan people" by forcing Catholicism down their throats.

They never "Christianized" the Native people, but left them with a bitter taste in their mouths. As a result, they are generally quite angry towards religion, which is understandable. This is not the love, forgiveness, or new life that the real Lord Jesus Christ gives to people. When I read the words below from Revelation 18:4–5, I knew they were speaking to me about renouncing all aspects of this false gospel:

> And I heard another voice from heaven saying, Come out of her, my people, that ye be not partakers of her sins, and that ye receive not any of her plagues. For her sins have reached unto heaven, and God hath remembered her iniquities.

Second Corinthians 4:4 tells us that Satan has blinded the minds of the unbelieving. Those who are spiritually blind cannot know true freedom or new life in Christ.

But whether we are believers or unbelievers, we have this in common: We have the same enemy, Satan. The devil hates mankind because he hates anything that is created in God's image, and he will do everything possible to hinder and destroy us, even while promising to bless us.

The great difference is that Christians have been born again and have been delivered from Satan's realm by the atoning death of Jesus Christ. They never again have to be subject to the devil's power. That's why it is so incredibly tragic when they fail to recognize when they are partakers in the works of darkness despite how the Bible continually urges them to test everything.

On the other hand, the unbeliever walks in darkness and has no real escape from Satan's realm and power unless he or she calls upon the name of the Lord Jesus Christ. God longs to deliver the unbeliever from Satan's grasp:

> To open their eyes, and to turn them from darkness to light, and from the power of Satan unto God, that they may receive forgiveness of sins, and inheritance among them which are sanctified by faith that is in me. (Acts 26:18)

There is hope for the unbeliever for Romans 10:13 tells us: "For whosoever shall call upon the name of the Lord shall be saved."

The charts on the following pages will help you understand the differences between a truly biblical outlook that springs from a true faith in Christ Jesus and Satan's counterfeit.

BIBLICAL VIEW VERSUS NATIVE SPIRITUALITY VIEW

CREATION OF THE WORLD

Biblical View	Native Spirituality View
God, the infinite, personal Creator, originally spoke into existence an all-together good spiritual material universe that He is still involved in and sovereignly controls (Genesis 1-2; Romans 1:25, 9:22, 14:9; Philippians 3:21; Psalm 104; 1 Timothy 4:4).	Many different unbiblical views of creation exist. Worship of creation is an earth-based spirituality in which those practicing Native Spirituality worship their ancestors and practice animism (worship of animals, rocks, trees, and other created entities).

FALL OF MANKIND

Biblical View	Native Spirituality View
Adam and Eve sinned, thus degenerating humanity and the world into a sinful, fallen state controlled by Satan and subject to death (Genesis 3; Ephesians 2:2; John 5:19).	Although Native Americans do believe in sin, they don't understand how or why humanity fell.

NATURE OF GOOD & EVIL	
Biblical View	**Native Spirituality View**
God is entirely good (1 John 1:5) and did not create evil (James 1:13-15). Evil results from rebellion against a perfectly righteous God. We are born into sin and are under God's judgment until Christ, God's Son, delivers us. Satan, in his pride, wanted to be like God and rebelled, but God cast him and his followers out of Heaven (2 Corinthians 5:10; 2 Peter 3:7 Ephesians 2:3; Revelation 20:11-15).	There are evil spirits and bad behavior, which must either be appeased or controlled. Those with animistic views embrace the idea that there are untold number of gods and spirits, both good and evil.

SIN & REDEMPTION

Biblical View	Native Spirituality View
Jesus Christ was born in the flesh, was crucified on the Cross for our sins, and was resurrected by the Father in Heaven. Those who trust in Him are born again and cleansed of their sins. As believers, we share in His death and resurrected life. (Romans 1-8)	There is a powerful distortion of sin and redemption in Roman Catholic teaching mixed in with Native Spirituality. Good and evil are viewed in much the same way as the belief of earning one's way to Heaven by doing good works. During a funeral, for instance, those who practice Native Spirituality usually perform some type of ceremony to assist the deceased in entering into Heaven. No one ever seems to go to Hell. Because they do not believe the Cross can redeem them from the punishment resulting from the wages of sin, they punish themselves with various attempts at purification. They do not see the inherent potential for evil that exists in relationships with demonic spirits. The sweat lodge represents an individual returning to the womb, suggestive of being born again. A woman's moontime suggests blood shedding. Both are counterfeits of Christ shedding His blood on the Cross for all of our sins so we might be born again.

VIEW OF LIFE

Biblical View	Native Spirituality View
The true meaning of life is encapsulated in a timeline and genealogy of human history that moves toward fulfillment and the return of Jesus Christ, followed by a new Heaven and a new Earth. Walk in the light with the Lord Jesus Christ, living for the glory of God and in loving fellowship with one another. God disciplines us to live in holiness and continues to forgive us of our sins as we seek Him and forgive those who sin against us (1 John 1:7-9; Hebrews 12:10).	Life is a circle—a cycle of birth, life, death, and rebirth represented by the medicine wheel. It includes spiritism, human sacrifices, sweat lodge ceremonies, sweet grass, pipe, sacred or healing ceremonies, witchcraft, sorcery, vision quests, necromancy, and other occult concepts and practices.

PROTECTION WHILE LIVING ON EARTH

Biblical View	Native Spirituality View
Countless verses in the Bible talk about God's protection for those who trust in Him, such as Psalm 18:30 and Psalm 5:11. The Father also sends His angels to guard those who are "heirs of salvation." (Psalm 91; Hebrews 1:14)	Native Spirituality teaches that each person is born with a particular spirit keeper that watches over him or her. These keepers represent animals and other elements of the earth. It also teaches that man should seek to appease spirits with offerings and wear medicine bags.

AFTERLIFE	
Biblical View	**Native Spirituality View**
Only those written in the Book of Life (born-again servants of the Lord Jesus Christ) will live with Him in glory forever—loving, serving, and enjoying Him (John 3, 17:24; Revelation 21-22). Blessed are they that do his commandments, that they may have right to the tree of life, and may enter in through the gates into the city. For without are dogs, and sorcerers, and whoremongers, and murderers, and idolaters, and whosoever loveth and maketh a lie. (Revelation 22:14-15)	A wide variety of beliefs exist about life after death—ranging from reincarnation in human or animal form to people becoming spirits. There are many rituals where practitioners attempt to contact spirit ancestors.

For thou hast trusted in thy wickedness: thou hast said, None seeth me. Thy wisdom and thy knowledge, it hath perverted thee; and thou hast said in thine heart, I am, and none else beside me. Therefore shall evil come upon thee; thou shalt not know from whence it riseth: and mischief shall fall upon thee; thou shalt not be able to put it off: and desolation shall come upon thee suddenly, which thou shalt not know. (Isaiah 47: 10-11)

Six

NEW AGE ELEMENTS IN NORTH AMERICAN NATIVE SPIRITUALITY

> Stand now with thine enchantments, and with the multitude of thy sorceries . . . Thou art wearied in the multitude of thy counsels. Let now the astrologers, the stargazers, the monthly prognosticators, stand up, and save thee from these things that shall come upon thee. (Isaiah 47: 12)

In the first edition of *Muddy Waters,* I used the term *neo-paganism* to denote the New Age/occult influences within Native Spirituality. In this new edition, I am going to be using the term New Age or New Spirituality interchangeably with neo-paganism. The terms are basically synonymous, but New Age incorporates an even broader scope of ideologies and practices. I like this explanation best:

> [Neo-paganism] carries some nuances of the revival of old paganism, but that is what the New Age is. So we stick to New Age and/or New Spirituality. Also New Age conveys the additional idea of creating or evolving into a new order on earth and that then brings in the eschatological factors. So it is more encompassing [than neo-paganism] and describes a purpose for the mystical revival.[1]

Just what is the New Age? One thing it is not, is new. It is actually a very old belief system dating back to ancient esoteric practices. Author and lecturer Ray Yungen has researched the New Age for nearly three decades. He explains the New Age this way:

> The term itself was taken from astrology making reference to the Aquarian age in which humanity is supposedly going to realize its inner divinity. Hence, anyone who engages in these mystical practices is associated with this view, even though they may have lived centuries ago.[2]

> Individuals who, in the context of historical occultism, are in mystical contact with unseen sources and dimensions; who receive guidance and direction from these dimensions, and most importantly, who *promote* this state-of-being to the rest of humanity.[3]

Often, talking about occult practices with people is difficult, even among many professing Christians who unfortunately fail to recognize there is a supernatural realm that includes very real evil and demonic forces. Because of this, it is hard to convince most people that mystical practices and occultism are anything but benign. They think such practices are purely fictional or science fiction—like a *Star Wars* movie. But the Bible tells us evil "principalities and powers" do indeed exist. With this in mind, let us now take a detailed look at some of the main New Age/New Spirituality elements that appear in North American Native Spirituality and what the Bible has to say about them.

WITCHCRAFT

> There shall not be found among you any one that maketh his son or his daughter to pass through the fire, or that useth divination, or an observer of times, or an enchanter, or a witch. Or a charmer, or a consulter with familiar spirits, or a wizard, or a necromancer.

> For all that do these things are an abomination unto the LORD: and because of these abominations the LORD thy God doth drive them out from before thee. (Deuteronomy 18:10–12)

> And I will cut off witchcrafts out of thine hand; and thou shalt have no more soothsayers. (Micah 5:12)

First Nations people often say that what they are doing is not bad since they are only involved in healing and not cursing others with witchcraft. But witchcraft is forbidden in the Bible, whether it is called black magic or white magic or given any other name.

Witchcraft involves the art of using magical (demonic) powers to accomplish one's will.[4] Many varieties have existed for centuries. In a book titled *Witchcraft Goes Mainstream*, the author states that modern religious witchcraft appeared in England in the 1940s and arrived in the United States in the 1950s and 1960s, to where it now "has become one of the most dynamic and rapidly growing movements in America."[5]

When we consider just how widespread witchcraft (or Wicca) has become, the following is very sobering:

> God has shown us that witchcraft, sorcery, magic, and sexual promiscuity breed addiction to those behaviors, separation from God, and spiritual death. Terrible bondage occurs, not because God inflicts it, but because the victims—having rejected God's protective love—bring it on themselves. In spite of popular illusions about nature's goodness, human nature tends to be self-centered rather than self-giving. Under the guidance and power of demonic spirits, it eventually becomes capricious, hateful, cruel, and deadly.[6]

NEO-PAGANISM

Neo-paganism is "a broad umbrella term for those who pursue or blend Wicca, Native American religions, New Age, and other contemporary forms of other earth-centered religions."[7] The neo-pagan (i.e., New Age) religious view is in stark contrast to the Bible. Its chief spiritual components are animism, polytheism, pantheism, feminism, rejection of the concept of sin and Christ's unique redemptive role (e.g. atonement, holiness, forgiveness), and the belief that we have no higher judge than ourselves.

Animism:

This doctrine teaches that a living *spiritual* element is connected to all matter, not just humans. It would include animals, rocks, trees, and the earth itself—alongside the premise that the nature of this spiritual element is divine.

Today there are around 2,500,000 Native Americans consisting of roughly 80 tribes speaking 50 different languages throughout the United States, yet:

> In all the Indian languages there is not the word "religion" . . . they speak about "tradition" . . . Each one has their own special tradition . . . but, in general, they do not speak about "gods," but about "spirits," with the "Great Spirit," "the Wise One Above" . . . but the Spirit comes through the air, and he is in everybody and everywhere . . . many animals have sacred powers, and must be protected as divine: Deer, buffalo, eagle, serpents, fox, bear, beaver . . . a favorite symbol of evil is the coyote . . . the sun, moon, sky, Mother Earth, and all therein and thereon are spirits to be worshiped.[8]

Polytheism:

This is a belief system that propagates the existence of more than one God. Buddhism, for instance, would be polytheistic, as it is teeming with hundreds of millions of gods. Traditional

Native American Spirituality focuses on the Great Spirit, but animism and polytheism dominate. There is a world of difference between saying there is One God whom we alone worship (as the Bible does) and worshiping one god among many. The verse below reads:

> See now that I, even I, am he, and there is no god with me: I kill, and I make alive; I wound, and I heal: neither is there any that can deliver out of my hand. (Deuteronomy 32:39)

And Isaiah 44:8 says, "Is there a God beside me? yea, there is no God; I know not any." As the Indian Bible College affirms:

> God will not share His glory with anything in creation. To do so is idolatry. To combine elements of Native religion and biblical truth is syncretism. We must renounce and avoid any form of idolatry and syncretism, because they are forbidden in Scripture.[9]

Indian Bible College then lists the following verses to back up their statement: Deuteronomy 32:39, Colossians 1:17-19, Ephesians 1:6,12,14, Hebrews 1:3-4, 1 Corinthians 10:31, Isaiah 42:8, Exodus 20:3-6, Romans 1:23, Colossians 3:5, 2 Kings 40:41, 2 Corinthians 6:14-17, 2 Corinthians 4:2, Acts 19:18-20, 1 Corinthians 5:11 and Isaiah 42:17.

Pantheism and Panentheism:

Pantheism sees God as a divine force of which all things consist. In other words, all things—man and creation—embody or ARE God.

Panentheism, on the other hand, is where God is IN all things. New Ager and founder of Creation Spirituality, Matthew Fox, says: "Divinity is found in all creatures. . . . The Cosmic Christ is the 'I am' in every creature."[10]

Feminism:

You may have heard of feminine spirituality or goddess spirituality. It is earth-centered, where "Mother Earth" is worshiped and revered. Native Spirituality fits well with the earth-centered approach.

Books like *The Shack* where God is portrayed as a woman and Sue Monk Kidd's book (and movie) *The Secret Life of Bees* have helped to escalate the goddess spirituality mindset in mainstream religion, including many Christian circles.[11]

AFTERLIFE

Among the world's religions, there are conflicting beliefs about life after death. For example, there is reincarnation where a person comes back over and over as either a different human or an animal, depending on their performance in the prior life. Another belief is that man's spirit is released after death and enters into union with a universal all-is-one energy or connection. And then, there are the agnostics and atheists who believe that after we die, nothing happens—we simply return to the dust from which we came.

No wonder Native Spirituality focuses on animals. There is no glorious eternal inheritance with Christ to look forward to and no greater purpose to life beyond this earth. Such spirituality is basically soulish and earthbound and therefore, devoid of hope of eternal life.

The Bible, God's inerrant Word, declares that God is Lord of both Heaven and earth (Luke 10:21). It lays out very clearly what is going to happen to man when he dies. It teaches that God will judge the dead, both great and small, and that if anyone's name is not found in the Book of Life (those who do not belong to Christ Jesus), they will be thrown into the lake of fire (Hebrews 9:27; Revelation 20:11-15).

> Blessed are they that do his commandments, that they may have right to the tree of life, and may enter in through the gates into the city. For without are dogs, and sorcerers, and whoremongers, and murderers, and idolaters, and whosoever loveth and maketh a lie. (Revelation 22:14-15)

The Lord Jesus Christ says:

> If a man abide not in me, he is cast forth as a branch, and is withered; and men gather them, and cast them into the fire, and they are burned. (John 15:6)

However, those who do abide in Him (those who are born-again through the shed blood of Jesus Christ) have Heaven to look forward to and will live with Him in glory forever (John 3; 17:24; Hebrews 9:28; Revelation 21–22). The Bible doesn't tell us everything about what Heaven will be like, but it does assure us there will be no more death, no more pain, and no more tears or sadness (Revelation 21:4). It also says:

> [A]s it is written, Eye hath not seen, nor ear heard, neither have entered into the heart of man, the things which God hath prepared for them that love him. (1 Corinthians 2:9)

When we consider that eternal life in Heaven is offered to every human being as a free gift for just believing on and trusting in the Lord Jesus Christ, it would be to our own detriment to reject such a gift.

ANCESTRAL SPIRITS

Former medicine man Cliff Schaeffer believes ancestral spirits are passed down intergenerationally through an [unsaved] family because someone in the family's past practiced Indian medicine or a black art. He states:

> Perhaps a family member fell under a curse where the spirits sent against him/her took root . . . Perhaps medicine powers were passed down unknowingly to a family member.[12]

In any event, many Native Americans, as well as some Christians, do believe in generational curses or the transmission of such demonic power through families. Some confusion exists in this area among Christians. I personally believe that rather than repenting of ties to ancestral spirits once we have become Christians we should repent of 'ancestral spirits' as a pagan belief system that is both false and oppressive. When Christ becomes Lord of our lives, all of that is washed away under His saving blood, and we become new creations.[13] Scripture does tell us that "For as in Adam all die," meaning we have inherited that sinful nature, but it also tells us, as believers in Christ: "[S]o also in Christ all shall be made alive" (1 Corinthians 15:22).

We are, however, called upon to repent of false worship or idolatry—that is, the worship of anything *other than* God, of which demon worship has become all too common in earth-centered spirituality. In the last chapter of this book, I do bring up the issue of repenting our past sins and involvements again.

In Corinthians, we find:

> But I say, that the things which the Gentiles sacrifice, they sacrifice to devils, and not to God: and I would not that ye should have fellowship with devils. Ye cannot drink the cup of the Lord, and the cup of devils: ye cannot be partakers of the Lord's table, and of the table of devils. (1 Corinthians 10:20-21)

The Bible teaches that ancestral spirits are really fallen angels or demons. These demons are not the spirits of dead persons, though they do pretend to be (i.e., spiritualism).

Those who live and die go to await judgment. Their spirits don't have the choice or the power to delay leaving.

> And as it is appointed unto men once to die, but after this the judgment: So Christ was once offered to bear the sins of many; and unto them that look for him shall he appear the second time without sin unto salvation. (Hebrews 9:27–28)

Animal Spirits

In Native Spirituality, there is the erroneous belief that animal spirits protect people or guide humans mainly in the supernatural realm. Medicine men or shamans often talk about how they visit someone without their knowledge by entering an animal spiritually.

Animal spirits can represent many things, but a couple examples of some popular beliefs are: the spirit of the bear is anger, destruction, greed, and fear; the spirit of the eagle represents power, pride, and haughtiness; the loon's spirit represents depression, suicide, and loneliness; and the spirit of the owl represents fear and even death.[14]

I often heard Grandpa, Dad, and many others speak about visitation from animals and birds who were other shamans either encouraging them or spying on them. And I recall medicine men being afraid of the bad luck the owls would supposedly bring when they saw or heard them nearby during their ceremonies. Some medicine men also use fish spirits, and some Natives actually believe that a loved one who has drowned turns into a fish—such as a salmon or a whale.

Nothing in the Bible supports these claims. Rather, it teaches that we must not exchange "the glory of the uncorruptible God into an image made like to corruptible man, and to birds, and four-footed beasts, and creeping things" (Romans 1:23). That would be idolatry. Idolatry basically means worshiping anything in God's place. The human heart has unlimited idols.[15]

But interaction with deceiving spirits through animal worship is not limited to Native American Spirituality. Today's widespread "New Spirituality" (which is interspiritual, panentheistic, and pantheistic) involves unmistakable connections between animal spirits, shamans, and some "neo-prophetic seers" and intercessors.[16]

Symbolic Child Sacrifices

The medicine men also made symbolic baby sacrifices to Satan for more spiritual power. Such sacrifices didn't actually involve killing the child physically and then offering it to Satan like some satanic cults do. Instead, a living child was offered to Satan in exchange for more spiritual powers. The child's life would then belong to the devil. An exchange was made in the form of a sacrificial offering. The child's life would then become filled with all kinds of evil works for the benefit of more spiritually dark powers given to the medicine man or woman. Most times the child doesn't even know that the demonic exchange has been made as it is made without his or her knowledge or consent. This is what happened to me and one reason why I had such a struggle when I became a Christian. Satan still claimed ownership of me. (The tug of war first started when I accepted the Lord Jesus Christ as my Lord and Savior.)

A relative confirmed this as definitely occurring as it also happened to one of her own children. Most of those "sacrificial offerings" get passed on in the days of one's youth. My late Grandpa John had also mentioned this a few times to us while I was visiting him at his house. I know personally of a woman who had used a love potion on a man twenty years her junior. When a love potion or a curse is sent, one must always sacrifice something. This woman sacrificed her children at a ghastly price. Most of her children have now died without knowing Jesus Christ as their Lord and Savior. Today, this same man is in a common-law relationship with one of the woman's surviving daughters.

CURSES OF THE BREATH

Curses are common in Native Spirituality. A curse by attachment may be a concoction in liquid or powder form attached to something like jewelry, cloth, or paper; or it is sometimes simply one blown by the breath. For instance, a sender may use a love potion to attract a member of the opposite sex or send a love potion or Indian medicine "by the breath" by blowing a curse into something like a voodoo doll or even onto a person through a handshake.

Potions and even medicine bags have different combinations of ingredients. Typically, medicine people use bird feathers, the most common being an eagle feather, because it represents power.

Other ingredients can be bear claws or teeth, different animal bones, intestines, tobacco, plants, herbs, roots, sweet grass, sage, willow tree bark, fungus, animal or bird gall bladders, and so on.

CREATION

What could be more important than our origin? What we believe about this vital area reveals what we think about ourselves, our purpose, our destiny—and our Creator.

Tribal myths of origin differ. One set of themes states that in the beginning many people populated the world, most of whom then became animals. This supposedly explains why Natives feel a close bond with animals.

This view of animals hinders Native Americans from realizing that God made us in His image and does not intend us to imitate animals but to rule them. The Bible reveals that the real creator of humanity is God, the Father of the Lord Jesus Christ, who is also the Master of humans.

> In the beginning God created the heavens and the earth. . . . And God said, Let us make man in our image, after our likeness: and let them have dominion over the fish of the sea, and over the fowl of the air, and over the cattle, and over all the earth, and over every creeping thing that creepeth upon the earth. (Genesis 1:1, 26)

DREAM CATCHERS

How about dream catchers—those spidery "sacred hoops" with feathers? They originated with the Ojibwa tribe during the '60s and '70s, supposedly to protect a sleeper by "catching" bad dreams or evil spirits. Then they caught on with other tribes and spread through the New Age movement into popular culture. Today, it is not uncommon to see dream catchers in gift and variety stores.

Dream catchers are even used in some public school settings, as the following describes:

> Every classroom displayed at least one dreamcatcher—a magical spider web inside a sacred circle. The students explained that dreamcatchers protect them from evil spirits and nightmares by catching the bad dreams but permitting good dreams to pass though the center. According to fourth grade teacher Ms. Preston, the amber crystal in the center of her dreamcatcher meant proper spiritual alignment with the energy of the universe.[17]

But you can be sure, most of the general public has no idea of the meaning and purpose of dream catchers.

Basically, using a dream catcher in its intended purpose is nothing more than a form of practicing occultism. How can an inanimate object "catch" evil spirits, much less bad dreams? And why attempt to "catch" evil spirits or nightmares when you cannot fight them physically?

Although Native people can sometimes see into the spiritual world of darkness, dream catchers, or anything having to do with the occult, merely attract evil spirits and demonic activity and provide no means of protection from them. Using dream catchers is an open invitation for more spiritual works of darkness.

If you are a born-again Christian, you have a Protector—God Almighty—Who stands between us and the evil realm. We need nothing more than Jesus Christ Himself who overcame all works and powers of darkness by His death and resurrection. If we pay attention to God's Word and not to seducing spirits, we can walk in His freedom from fear.

Ephesians 6:12 says that our battle is not against "flesh and blood," but is against "principalities," "powers," "the rulers of the darkness" and "spiritual wickedness in high places." And in Hebrews, we read:

> Forasmuch then as the children are partakers of flesh and blood, he also himself likewise took part of the same; that through death he might destroy him that had the power of death, that is, the devil; And deliver them who through fear of death were all their lifetime subject to bondage. (Hebrews 2:14–15)

Medicine Bags

Medicine bags are small bags, usually of leather or cloth, which Native people wear around their waists or their necks for spiritual strengthening and for protection against evil influences. Each bag has unique contents; they may be herbs, stones, feathers, or some item related to that person's spirit keeper (see section on spirit keepers).

In Native Spirituality, people reverence these bags not only for their value as protection but because they act as reminders of their spiritual walks. Some Natives relate it to the cross that some Christians wear around their necks. The demonic counterfeiting of these bags to the cross is obvious.

As I mentioned earlier, my grandfather, who was a medicine man, used to make such "protection" for all of his descendants. But all it did was attract demons. There is no real protection from evil outside of the Cross of Christ Jesus.

Medicine Wheel

Native Americans developed the concept of the medicine wheel to illustrate their belief that life is a circle—from birth to death to rebirth—and to act as a guide to understanding self, creation, and their duties. Everything within the wheel is interrelated, and the goal is that these interconnected elements are in balance with each other. Important ceremonies always take place within a circle.

Four is a significant number within Native Spirituality—four directions, four winds, four seasons, four elements, and so forth.

Hence, the wheel has four quadrants, which move in a clockwise direction because that is the sun's direction.

There are numerous interpretations and uses of the wheel, but the following is the one my own family used. We believed our spirit keeper was the grizzly bear:

In the center are the creator and the individual. East represents beginning or birth, spring, and where the sun rises and is symbolized by the eagle as spirit keeper. The next quadrant, the south, is the mental area, representing the teenage years and symbolized by the buffalo as spirit keeper. The west represents the emotions as well as the season of fall and is symbolized by the grizzly bear. The north represents the spiritual self and is symbolized by the wolf.

Francis Whiskeyjack, a Cree elder and expert on the medicine wheel states:

> As we share in this circle with others, we are asking the Creator, the healer, to heal us. We are asking our spirit guides, the helpers, our grandfathers and grandmothers, to pray for us, to be mediators and to help us.[18]

The Wheel summarizes their earth-centered faith and reveals a system of interaction of animistic, pantheistic, and spiritualistic beliefs in their search for spiritual wholeness.

This is only a brief summary of a very complex teaching that has had great influence for centuries among Native American peoples.

A Native American Medicine Wheel

Contrary to this view, however, the biblical view is linear. That is, it views human life as having a beginning and an end. From the creation to the return of Jesus Christ, from the fall of man in Genesis to the new Heaven and the new earth, God reveals in the Bible a linear history filled with purpose: to create a new people for Himself. The medicine wheel indicates that there is no beginning and no end to the existence of a man or other created beings. But we know from Scripture that carnal man does indeed have a beginning (birth) and an end (death). Likewise, in linear fashion, those who are written in the Book of Life will live eternally in Heaven based on the finished work at the Cross by Jesus Christ while everlasting Hell awaits those who reject Christ.

The medicine wheel is used to make contact with the dead, with spirit guides, and with the "great spirit." But the Bible is clear that man has only one mediator between him and God:

> For there is one God, and one mediator between God and men, the man Christ Jesus. (1 Timothy 2:5).

NATIVE ART AND JEWELRY

If you type in the term "Native American Jewelry" into Google, it comes up about 740,000 times. Type in "Native American Art," and that comes up over three million times. Needless to say, Native American jewelry and art have become very popular. The former medicine man, now Christian believer, Cliff Schaeffer tells about the significance that art and jewelry hold in Native Spirituality:

> Most native artists receive their inspiration from the "spirits" and therefore they pray before the creation of the artwork or jewelry and they give thanks and dedicate it after its creation. Most uninformed Christians see nothing wrong with owning elaborately painted drums, Dream Catchers, Eagle feathers or some types of silver jewelry, rock jewelry or paintings and drawings.
>
> These items cannot be possessed by demons, but they certainly can attract them, and attracting demons into [one's] home can lead to spiritual oppression. Acts 19:19 shows new Christians who have come out of sorcery burning their scrolls. This type of jewelry and art also

> tends to offend Christians who have come out of that sort of background and who know what the spiritual implications are.[19]

This is not to say that all jewelry and artwork made by Native Americans has been dedicated to spirits; but in such cases where it has, this creates an open invitation to the forces of darkness. Once again, the Native American who practices Native Spirituality does this to have spiritual protection, but in so doing, imparts a connection or association that the demonic realm and those familiar with it recognize.

NECROMANCY

The practice of necromancy is divination by alleged communication with the dead. When medicine men go into the sweat lodges, they summon and talk with what they believe are their dead ancestors to ask for guidance, direction, or healing. Yet, in reality, they communicate with familiar spirits or spirit guides who know intimate details about each person they are assigned to, usually without their knowledge. These spirits are what may come to you in your dreams, or you may hear their voices. In some cases, they may pose as loved ones who have passed on.

Native elders, or their followers, often become angry when there are Christians present, and in some cases they ask them to leave. If they truly worship the one and only true God, why then do they get angry or ask Christians to leave? The real explanation is that there are two opposing forces at war—God and Satan. The real reason why Christians are asked to leave the area is that the devil is afraid that Christ's truth will expose his lies.

Medicine men, and those who practice necromancy, are speaking to and worshiping demons, which is why they become angry when Christians question them; they think that Christians are disrespecting their beliefs. Instead, they should be asking, "Could it be that the truth is making me angry?" Christians are right to reject these beliefs. In fact, they shouldn't even be in such a session in the first place.

The Bible states there is a great chasm that prevents any type of visitation from beyond. Luke 16:26 says:

> And beside all this, between us and you there is a great gulf fixed: so that they which would pass from hence to you cannot; neither can they pass to us, that would come from thence.

Once when we were left home alone, I stayed up until about four a.m. hoping Dad would come home. I finally fell asleep and had a dream that I had died and could feel my soul floating upwards out of my body. It was very seductive because it felt beautiful, and there was music unlike anything I had ever heard. I was gone about five or six minutes, and then a voice said I had to go back because it was not my time. Even after I came to the Lord, I believed this for a while. Then I finally repented of it because of its association with necromancy. A Christian must have nothing to do with such a work of darkness!

Sometimes healing takes place in such situations, but it definitely is not the Lord Jesus Christ doing the healing because these beliefs and practices are clearly an abomination to Him. Only Satan would have the power to heal at a sweat lodge ceremony. Yes, the devil can bring temporary healing, but it is always for the purpose of further ensnaring a person into the works of darkness. The Bible warns of such false miracles, signs, and wonders in Revelation 13:14 and 16:14. And as for attempting to communicate with the dead, the Bible clearly warns:

> There shall not be found among you any one that maketh his son or his daughter to pass through the fire, or that useth divination, or an observer of times, or an enchanter, or a witch. Or a charmer, or a consulter with familiar spirits, or a wizard, or a necromancer.

> For all that do these things are an abomination unto the LORD: and because of these abominations the LORD thy God doth drive them out from before thee. Thou shalt be perfect with the LORD thy God. For these nations, which thou shalt possess, hearkened unto observers of times, and unto diviners: but as for thee, the LORD thy God hath not suffered thee so to do. (Deuteronomy 18:10–14)

The idea that we can communicate with the dead and they can communicate with us has begun to drift into the Christian church. In Larry Debruyn's book review of *Have Heart* (written by a pastor who lost his son in a car accident), Mr. Debruyn states:

> I fear, with the growing emphasis on reports of Christians visiting Heaven, or of receiving visits from Heaven, whether solicited or not, that the evangelical church is stepping onto the "slippery slope" leading to spiritualism and spiritism, something practiced by the Canaanites and forbidden by God's Law. . . .
>
> Spiritualism is very attractive because it promises knowledge of the future and communication with dead loved ones. Many people will be influenced by demonic spirits in this way without realizing it. . . . "God has forbidden humans to try to communicate with the departed dead; such attempts result in communication with deceitful spirits, known as 'familiar' spirits. . . ." The spirits are called "familiar" because people think they know them from life![20]

Paying the Spirits

Paying the spirits is a method of offering a gift to the spirits in exchange for guidance, wisdom, or understanding, or perhaps to find a lost item or person. A sum of money, cloth, blankets or anything of value can act as a gift. Some pay with cars or horses.

It is thought that the more generous the gift, the more powerful the medicine or supernatural help.

Tobacco is the most popular gift used to seek protection from harm, unfavorable weather, bad health, or to obtain good luck in trapping animals and in fur trading. Some people often try to combat unfavorable weather by tying a pouch of tobacco to the end of a pole and positioning it to point toward an approaching storm in order to divert the storm's course.

You can be absolutely certain that any answers come from demons playing the role of the person's imagined god. See how subtle Satan's deception is? These practices are not of God and therefore, are in vain. The gift of forgiveness and eternal life in the Lord Jesus Christ is free; He does not cost a horse; He does not cost anything.

> Ho, every one that thirsteth, come ye to the waters, and he that hath no money; come ye, buy, and eat; yea, come, buy wine and milk without money and without price. (Isaiah 55:1)

> For the wages of sin is death; but the gift of God is eternal life through Jesus Christ our Lord. (Romans 6:23)
> Take my yoke upon you, and learn of me . . . For my yoke is easy, and my burden is light. (Matthew 11: 29-30)

PEYOTE AND THE NATIVE AMERICAN CHURCH

As mentioned before, there are many syncretistic mixtures and modifications of traditional Native American Spirituality these days. The largest organized such mixture is the Native American Church. Its eighty chapters and membership of 250,000 incorporate "generic Native American religious rites, Christianity, and the use of the peyote plant.[21] The modern peyote ritual is comprised of four parts: praying, singing, eating peyote, and quietly contemplating."[22]

According to an article written by the University of Virginia:

> The Native American Church, or Peyote Church, illustrates a trend of modifying and manipulating traditional Native American spirituality. The Native American Church incorporates Christianity, as well as moving away from tribal specific religion. . . . And in the last few decades, New Age spirituality has continued the trend.[23]

Notice the syncretistic combining of Christianity with paganism in the following statement about the Huichol Indians of northwestern Mexico:

> Huichol religion parallels Christianity in that the Creator, out of compassion for his people, subjects himself to the limitations of this world. In Christianity he incarnates himself as a man who dies but is resurrected to save human beings; in Huichol belief he dies and is reborn in the Peyote plant to give his people wisdom.
>
> The Aztecs are the cultural cousins of the Huichol, and their word peyotl or peyutl denotes the pericardium, the envelope or covering of the heart. This corresponds strictly to the Huichol belief that Peyote embodies the Creator's heart.[24]

First of all, peyote is a hallucinogenic drug that opens those who ingest it to a non-biblical mystical realm governed by familiar spirits or demons. It is interesting to note that a Catholic mystic, Thomas Merton, once likened a psychedelic drug trip to practicing eastern-style meditation.[25] This is because the results of each are the same.

While it is true that Jesus Christ subjected Himself to the limitations of this world, and incarnated in order to rescue sinful human souls through His death and resurrection, there is absolutely no truth to the claim that He is reborn in the peyote plant

Quanah Parker, a Kwahadi Comanche chief, holding a Peyote feather fan. Parker was influential in the creation of the Native American Church.

to give wisdom. "This wisdom descendeth not from above, but is earthly, sensual, devilish" (James 3:15).

The danger in drug or meditation-induced mystical experiences is that the experience is a pseudo Holy Spirit. In other words, the practitioner will "feel" as though he or she is very close to God when in these altered states and therefore believe that the experiences, and the means by which they are induced (e.g., drugs or meditation), are good. But the Bible tells us that Satan comes as an angel of light and his demons are transformed as ministers of righteousness (2 Corinthians 11:14-15). It also tells us to test the spirits, meaning there are evil ones:

> Beloved, believe not every spirit, but try the spirits whether they are of God. (1 John 4:1)

POTLATCHES

According to Webster's Dictionary, a potlach is:

> [A] ceremonial feast of the American Indians of the northwest coast marked by the host's lavish distribution of gifts or sometimes destruction of property to demonstrate wealth and generosity with the expectation of eventual reciprocation.[30]

The Potlaches are a venue where many elements of Native Spirituality are practiced, including rituals and dancing. The Potlach is where a redistribution of wealth takes place, and in Canada and the United States was actually outlawed at one time, seen as kind of a "primitive communism."[31]

Spiritual ceremonies are always hidden behind the word "celebration" in these events, which creates a major problem for participation in them by Christians. The Bible warns Christians against having fellowship with those who call themselves Christians but who are behaving immorally or practicing idolatry:

> But now I have written unto you not to keep company, if any man that is called a brother be a fornicator, or covetous, or an idolator, or a railer, or a drunkard, or an extortioner; with such an one no not to eat. (1 Corinthians 5:11)

Powwows

A powwow is a gathering of North American Native people for a ceremony (such as victory in war) or a social event that usually includes competitive dancing. Derived from the Narragansett Algonquian word pauau, its original meaning was a gathering of medicine men, but later became a gathering of people to celebrate an important event.[32]

Some put on powwows to commemorate the passing on of a loved one. A memorial feast usually accompanies it to strengthen the loved one for the journey to Heaven. Salteaux Indians prepare their dead for their spiritual journey by making a fire that they burn 24 hours a day for the duration of the wake and funeral. They also cover the deceased's entire body with a blanket then they smudge themselves with sweet grass to view it. The significance of this act suggests the need for purification. During a powwow:

> [T]he eagle whistle is blown to honor the dancers, the drums, the spirit helpers, and the spirit of the eagle. Each time the whistle is blown a fitting song is sung.[33]

Over the years, I have tried to attend powwows, but even before I became a believer, I never felt comfortable at them. There was always a haunting sense of eeriness, and deep within I felt repulsed by the drumming and the chanting. I am grateful that Dad never forced us to follow those beliefs but left it for us to decide.

Unfortunately, even though some of us children may not have engaged in Native Spirituality or accepted any part of the teaching, we were not exempted from bondages because of our presence at such events, or simply because of the familial spirit keepers that befell our lineage after someone made a pact.

Now when I hear powwow music, my spirit recoils, and I know without a doubt that it is because there are spiritual forces of darkness at work. Some people, even some Christians, believe there are two different kinds of powwows—one used only for entertaining tourists and the other for traditional competitions. Frankly, it makes no difference to the spirit world which version is used as long as there are drums and chanting. Grandpa John said, "These came from the world of darkness after someone had a vision in the early 1800s and received them." Because of the origin of the vision, the demons now have an open door to enter one's life simply because of participation.

There is no possible way one can journey to Heaven through the rituals and dancing performed at powpows, for it is only through the acceptance of the risen Lord Jesus Christ as one's Lord and Savior that one will enter the kingdom of God. Sadly, the powwow is "an important vehicle for passing down the Indian traditions from one generation to the next."[34]

SACRED BUNDLES

The purpose of sacred bundles is to bring peace of mind. The bundles contain a variety of items, such as a smudge bowl, herbs, small stones, sweet grass, matches, feathers, flags or cloth, and tobacco ties, wrapped in cloth, leather, or a blanket, or in a box. Sometimes the bundle contains the owner's hair, which she or he cuts at the death of a loved one or as an act of repentance. Tobacco ties are small offerings of tobacco folded inside a cloth and sometimes saved for use in a future ceremony.

How sad and how tragic to have to look to inanimate objects for peace of mind when the living God reaches out with His love through the resurrected Jesus Christ, longing to save and to bring true peace of mind as His Word says numerous times. God's peace, the peace described in the Bible is free for the asking:

> Look unto me, and be ye saved, all the ends of the earth: for I am God, and there is none else. (Isaiah 45:22)
>
> Therefore being justified by faith, we have peace with God through our Lord Jesus Christ: By whom also we have access by faith into this grace wherein we stand, and rejoice in hope of the glory of God. (Romans 5:1–2)
>
> Thou wilt keep him in perfect peace, whose mind is stayed on thee: because he trusteth in thee. (Isaiah 26:3)
>
> And the peace of God, which passeth all understanding, shall keep your hearts and minds through Christ Jesus. (Philippians 4:7)

Sacred or Healing Circle

Sacred or healing circles resemble the pipe ceremony and exist to help people find healing or guidance, to share their feelings in a situation of accepting brotherhood or to receive teaching from the elders. They normally begin with a pipe ceremony as a means of removing any "negative energy" and to bring everyone into prayerful spiritual alignment. An eagle feather is passed to anyone who wants to speak, and no one can interrupt during that time.

While some healing can certainly take place on a soulish level as a result of the non-judgmental acceptance of feelings and problems, true spiritual unity can only occur when all present are washed by the blood of the crucified Lord Jesus Christ of all sin and are one in Christ. This means walking together in the unity and love of the Holy Spirit and the truth of the Word of God.

> If we say that we have no sin, we deceive ourselves, and the truth is not in us. If we confess our sins, he is faithful and just to forgive us our sins, and to cleanse us from all unrighteousness. (1 John 1:8–9)

> For as the body is one, and hath many members, and all the members of that one body, being many, are one body: so also is Christ. For by one Spirit are we all baptized into one body, whether we be Jews or Gentiles, whether we be bond or free; and have been all made to drink into one Spirit. (1 Corinthians 12:12–13)

SACRED PIPE CEREMONY

The great chiefs used the sacred pipe to seal peace treaties with the white man, viewing it as their version of the Holy Bible.

Grandpa John's understanding of the pipe's symbolism is that each bit of the "sacred tobacco" represents a part of all the created objects in this universe. The fire used to light the pipe supposedly symbolizes the "Great Spirit." The smoke that is inhaled inside represents the Great Spirit in that person; and as the smoke is blown out it means unification of God, the human, and the world takes place. This sacrifice is seen as a merging of all into harmony and balance. All powers of earth are merging into one in the inhaled smoke (when it is burning). This explains why Natives who practice Native Spirituality put such an emphasis on harmony and balance. One advocate for this states:

> The pipe bowl is symbolic of the female and the wooden pipe stem symbolizes the male. The joining of the two represents the connection between Mother Earth and all the creatures that inhabit Earth.[26]

Cliff Schaeffer explains:

> Out of all the elements, tobacco is the best means by which the spirits are attracted. . . . Once the spirits had been attracted, they then smoked in the company of those gathered and having done so, they were obligated to listen to the requests and to agree to them. This ceremony is also performed as an offering to the spirits.[27]

This nature symbolism doesn't recognize the distinction between the Creator and the creation, which is one of the foundational differences between Christian theism and pagan pantheism. The concept of Mother Earth (or goddess spirituality) is extremely common in earth-based religions throughout the pagan world as well as in the occult, such as the Jewish Kabbala. No such symbolism appears anywhere in the Bible. There is no "Mother God" (or Mother Earth) in Judeo-Christianity. And yet, goddess spirituality has really taken root within mainstream Western society. A popular film, based on the book by goddess spiritualist Sue Monk Kidd, *The Secret Life of Bees*, has an underlying theme of the goddess within;[28] so does William Paul Young's *New York Times* best seller *The Shack*. That book has been widely accepted by evangelical/Protestant Christianity. Much of the environmentalist movement is tied in with this spirituality too.[29]

How should the Christian respond? As mentioned earlier in this book, but which is well worth repeating, 1 Corinthians 10:20–21 clearly tells us that "the things which the Gentiles sacrifice, they sacrifice to devils, and not to God."

SHAMANISM

Basically, shamanism is the belief system that utilizes *shamans* in order to make contact with the spirit world. According to the *Encyclopedia of New Age Beliefs* (Harvest House), traditional shamanism "is where the shaman functions as healer, spiritual leader, and mediator between the spirits and people."[35]

Shamanism is found in most cultures. In Western society, Native Spirituality is the main venue, but it is not confined to Native Spirituality. The New Age movement began incorporating shamanistic rituals into their own New Age spirituality:

> New Agers have felt attracted to shamanism for a variety of reasons. A major factor in this attraction is that, while the shaman is a kind of mystic, the focus is on the forces of nature rather than an otherworldy mysticism. . . . Other attractions are the use of mind-altering drugs, including peyote, and the romanticized images of nature. [36]

Within Native Spirituality, shamans depend heavily upon drumming, singing, dancing, and chanting in order to get spirits to enter them and to help them. What many people probably do not realize is that shamanism is very dangerous.

In biblical terms, shamanism is the use of supposed spirit guides to attain spiritual power, knowledge, and healing, but the cost is ghastly, and the "dangers of shamanistic initiation"[37] are many. Some of these dangers and symptoms would be identical to what happens in Kundalini, which is a dangerous and powerful energy coming from deep meditation. This list shows what can happen when demonic realms are accessed through deep meditation practices in Native Spirituality, shamanism, and the New Age movement. Shockingly, Christians are now practicing this occultic meditation through the contemplative prayer movement:

1. Burning hot or ice cold streams moving up the spine.
2. Perhaps a feeling of air bubbles or snake movement up through the body.
3. Pains in varying locations throughout the body.
4. Tension or stiffness of neck, and headaches.
5. Feeling of overpressure within the head.

6. Vibrations, unease, or cramps in legs and other parts of the body.
7. Fast pulse and increased metabolism.
8. Disturbance in the breathing—and/or heart function.
9. Parapsychological abilities. Light phenomena in or outside the body.
10. Problems with finding balance between strong sexual urges, and a wish to live in sublime purity.
11. Persistent anxiety or anxiety attacks, due to lack of understanding of what is going on.
12. Insomnia, manic high spirits or deep depression. Energy loss.
13. Impaired concentration and memory.
14. Total isolation due to inability to communicate inner experiences out.
15. Experiences of possession and poltergeist phenomena.[38]

Other dangers would include insanity and psychosis. What's more, the use of shamanism in contemporary culture is widespread and the results are often devastating:

> [S]hamanism often involves the shaman in tremendous personal suffering and pain (magically, he often 'dies' in the most horrible of torments) . . . it often involves the shaman in demon possession, insanity, sexual perversion, and so on.[39]

Such a terrifying perversion of God's merciful ways is completely unnecessary, for Christ gives the Holy Spirit—the Spirit of love and goodness—to all who call upon His name and put their trust in Him (Romans 5:5).

Colossians 2:9-10 states the truth for Christians:

> For in him [the Lord Jesus Christ] dwelleth all the

> fulness of the Godhead bodily. And ye are complete in him, which is the head of all principality and power."

SMUDGING CEREMONY

Native Americans often depend upon a smudging ceremony to purify mind, body, and spirit, to eliminate negative thoughts, and to prepare for prayer. New Age practitioners also use these methods. Sage, sweet grass, tobacco, and certain types of fungus, cedar, and juniper are the most common ingredients, along with an eagle feather. The participant then fans the smoke over the body.

Large gatherings also use this ceremony to seek unification prior to some important activity like negotiations or conferences.

The New Testament teaches no such techniques for purification. The only cleansing it talks about is the cleansing from sin and evil, which only comes from repentance and the cleansing Christ's shed blood brings.

> Woe unto you, scribes and Pharisees, hypocrites! for ye make clean the outside of the cup and of the platter, but within they are full of extortion and excess. (Matthew 23:25)

SPIRIT KEEPERS

Native American Spirituality teaches that every Native born on Mother Earth comes with a spirit keeper for guidance and protection. These keepers represent animals, birds, plants, fish, and other aspects of creation. Natives compare these spirit keepers to the Christian concept of guardian angels.

The Bible talks about both spirits and angels, and they are not necessarily the same thing at all. Spirits of animals, birds, and so on sound like demons in disguise, whereas the purpose of good angels is clear: "Are they not all ministering spirits, sent forth to minister for them who shall be *heirs of salvation*?" (Hebrews 1:14; italics added). Spirit keepers do not lead their charge to salvation.

It is important to show how these spirit guides operate to gain further access into an unbeliever's life, so here's an example from my family.

During the mid '70s, an unholy spirit visited Dad every spring for a number of years. It asked him to accept it as his spirit guide. It said if he didn't, it would kill his kids one by one. Dad gathered us all together to inform us what had transpired and wanted to know if he should accept this spirit. We told him that he should reject it, and he did. When my brother was murdered in 1978, Dad accepted this spirit guide for fear it would kill the rest of us. This spirit appeared as a rattlesnake, and through occultic dreams, Dad saw its image as follows: Its head stuck out of the earth on the left side while its body wove through the earth to the bottom, then in and out of the earth again, with its tail finally sticking out on the right side—a perfect picture of 'the god of this world.' The god of this world was making his own altar calls.

SUN DANCES AND RENEWAL CELEBRATIONS

Sun dances and the renewal celebrations take place within Native Spirituality for many different reasons, but basically they are to give thanks, to pray for the renewal of the people, renewal of the earth, and to allow for socializing with old friends and meeting new people.

An individual can request the ceremony for supernatural help or because he has had a vision. Sun gazes denote confinement, evasion, torment. These worshippers inflict pain on themselves believing that they have to suffer for cleansing or for supernatural aid. They pierce holes in their chests or back muscles and then loop string or rope through the pierced skin with its end tied to a sacred lodge or to a sacred dance pole; they then tear away. Even though this particular practice has ceased, the sun dance can go on for days, sometimes involving sleep deprivation, which is known for inducing altered states of consciousness.

One Christian researcher, who has studied the Indigenous* People's Movement extensively, explains his concerns:

> I have great sympathy for the plight of the American Indian and the factors that have led to many problems because of past exploitation. But this does not mean that God "heard the prayers" of godless heathen. Crazy Horse and Sitting Bull may have been praying but certainly not to YHWH.... Sitting Bull summoned the Lakota, Cheyenne and Arapaho to his camp on Rosebud Creek in Montana Territory. There he led them in the sun dance ritual, offering prayers to Wakan Tanka, their Great Spirit, and slashing his arms one hundred times as a sign of sacrifice. Wakan Tanka is not YHWH. The dances of pagans to their gods are often signified by arm slashing (1 Kings 18:28).[40]

What a tragedy! They suffer needlessly because the Lord Jesus Christ already suffered for us and paid the full penalty for our sins when He bled and died on the Cross for our sins. The sun dance is a mockery of Isaiah 53:5:

> But he was wounded for our transgressions, he was bruised for our iniquities: the chastisement of our peace was upon him; and with his stripes we are healed.

His last words as He was giving up His spirit on the Cross were "It is finished!" (John 19:30). So there is no reason for anyone to punish himself by suffering in any manner for the cleansing of sin. The blood of the crucified Lord Jesus Christ can purify us completely.

Although Christ did it all, and the entire process of salvation is a gift of God (Romans 10:17), people continue to believe the lie that we need to do something (works) ourselves to receive blessings or to get to Heaven, such as inflicting pain during a sun dance

---

* Indigenous means any ethnic group of people who are originally from a particular place or country (e.g. the Inuits and Métis' are indigenous people of Canada.)

ceremony or some other form of suffering. Roman Catholicism and Native Spirituality both teach that we will get to Heaven if we do good works and/or suffer.

The Bible states in Ephesians 2:8–9:

> For by grace are ye saved through faith; and that not of yourselves: it is the gift of God: Not of works, lest any man should boast.

SWEAT LODGE CEREMONIES

The sweat lodge is an important part of Native Spirituality. The lodge may be a small structure made of a frame of saplings, covered with skins, canvas, or blanket and resembling a sauna. Or it may be a large one that can accommodate as many as a dozen or more people. Inside, they splash water onto hot rocks in a shallow pit in the middle to make steam.

The medicine man or the facilitator of the sweat lodge sets the time for each session, which usually varies from half an hour to forty-five minutes. When the sweating starts, the elder invites the spirits into the sweat lodge. The door to the sweat lodge is always facing the east because this is where the sun resides. They never allow a woman in her menstrual cycle to enter during the ceremonies. They say she is in her "moon-time" and fear that power in her blood is present, which will cause the medicine man to weaken. (Here we see a mockery of the power of the blood of the crucified and risen Lord Jesus Christ.)

Sweat lodge ceremonies are done in complete darkness; this represents an individual returning to the womb and is suggestive of being born again. Their purposes differ in many ways: spiritual cleansing and renewal, healing, educating the youth, asking for guidance or direction in life, or making a spiritual offering.

Purification rituals also use the sweat lodge ceremony to start or end vision quests. And "to receive spirits, an individual first has to be clean both internally and externally, which is achieved by . . . bathing in a sweat lodge."[41]

c. 1869—Little Big Mouth, a medicine man, seated in front of his [sweat] lodge near Fort Sill, Oklahoma, with medicine bag visible from behind the tent. National Archives

The medicine man or woman chants and prays repeatedly, calling upon animal, bird, or ancestral spirits to enter the sweat lodge. Different lineages have different spirits. In our lineage, the animal spirit was represented by the grizzly bear; the bird spirit is the eagle, and the ancestral spirits are referred to as "grandfathers" or "grandmothers." The medicine men or women encourage spirits to occupy their bodies during public ceremonies. Other times they require these spirits to leave and to perform necessary acts. They sometimes go into trances to seek healing or lost items.

People used to come to my grandfather John's place for healing through a sweat lodge ceremony. Sometimes it was because someone had cursed them through witchcraft or because someone was sick. A few wanted healing and freedom from substance abuse, but it never worked. Some even became worse, going into deeper bondage.

On one of my many visits home to my paternal grandpa John and my dad, Dad told me that he had been a sergeant at arms (doorkeeper) for Grandpa John when they held sweat lodge ceremonies in various locations. Once when they were in Saskatchewan, Canada, in the middle of nowhere, Dad was waiting for the ceremony to end when he noticed two Caucasian teenagers walking in a semi-circle. As he watched them, they walked directly in front of him, turned into snakes, and slithered into the sweat lodge. Another time, he says he saw a deer do the same thing. I believe this was God's way of showing Dad that sweat lodge ceremonies are evil. And, in fact, Dad told me that's when he realized the ceremonies are the devil's work.

Unfortunately, Dad didn't quit at that point but instead became an apprentice through my grandfather, John. Because Grandpa knew he wouldn't live much longer, he handed down the dark supernatural powers to Dad. I'm sure that if someone had explained the truth to Dad, he most likely would have quit. But God never gave up on him, and today he belongs to Jesus Christ instead of the devil.

In these ceremonies, we again see Satan's counterfeit, as this type of purification is nowhere found in the New Testament. Only the blood of the crucified and risen Jesus Christ can purify us of our sins. The worst thing is that Native people do believe they are worshiping the true God and are expecting to go to Heaven when they die. And to make matters worse, Roman Catholic teaching is frequently combined with Native Spirituality, which focuses the Natives upon works rather than Jesus Christ. Like many, I ignorantly endorsed both teachings until someone shared the Gospel with me, and I was born again through the Lord Jesus Christ. Our mighty God does not come in a wafer as the Catholic Church teaches![42]

> And this is the condemnation, that the light has come into the world, and men loved darkness rather than light, because their deeds were evil. (John 3:19)

Thunder Spirits

A former medicine man reveals further insight into the extent of polytheism and idolatry in Native Spirituality beliefs. Although his recollections are a bit different from my own memory of the four different thunders that Dad and Grandpa used to talk about, they are well worth recording. He tells us that:

> Thunder spirits are powers called upon more than any other power and is [*sic*] a multiple power residing in the four directions. Each direction is associated with a different color and cloths (flags) of that color are offered to the thunderers. The chief of the thunders resides above, to the east is the red thunder, to the south is the white thunder, to the west is blue thunder, and to the north is black thunder. Each direction also has a different animal spirit. Each of the four directions also has a special meaning associated with it. The four directions again are not exhaustive; they may also mean different things for each direction. They are as follows:

- EAST—the place of new beginnings, rebirth, childhood, new light.
- SOUTH—the place of youth, of action, the place habitual thinking seeks embodiment.
- WEST—the darkening place, the place of the bear, where self evaluation is carried out, the place of the vision quest.
- NORTH—the place of wisdom, clear knowledge of self, the place of Elder-hood where lessons learned become clear, the jumping off into the spirit world place.[43]

Vision Quests

A vision quest is a ceremonial rite of passage designed to mark life changes and is frequently part of shamanism. It may occur under the guidance of an older shaman or alone in the wilderness; it includes fasting and meditation to aid inner transformation.

Young children are often encouraged to go on vision quests. Prior to going, they "receive guidance about which spirit they are to seek."[44] According to one source, "If the quest is successful, the child is not supposed to acknowledge it publicly until he or she is older. It is also important that young people call upon the aid of the newly-acquired power only in serious situations."[45]

Similar to shamanistic initiations, the dangers of this kind of quest are innumerable.

Summary

You don't need to be directly involved in the occult, witchcraft, or divination and such for the rulers of darkness to harass and try to control your life. You don't even need to believe they're bad. All it takes is just even a little dabbling, which they see as entering their world. Out of ignorance, I've looked into a pool of badger blood to determine my life span and have seen others do it as well. But being ignorant did not protect me from the consequences of divination or from other aspects of my occult heritage of Native American Spirituality.

Those who have not been born again into the Lord Jesus Christ cannot escape the kingdom of darkness without the grace of God for they are "children of wrath" following "the course of this world, according to the prince of the power of the air, the spirit that now worketh in the children of disobedience" (Ephesians 2:2–3).

Only Christ has defeated Satan and his kingdom. And only Christ can bestow new life. Should we not turn "to God from idols to serve the living and true God" (1 Thessalonians 1:9)?

Even born-again Christians can be fooled, confused, or ignorant and become involved in occultism without realizing it.

Even born-again Christians can be fooled, confused, or ignorant and become involved in occultism without realizing it (witness the great confusion nowadays among Christians about the blatant witchcraft in the Harry Potter novels). While they ultimately belong to the Lord Jesus Christ, if they dabble in the occult, there are serious and evil consequences they may suffer.

Sometimes, we suffer from our foolishness. But although we may have to endure much suffering, He does promise that He will never forsake us and will use even evil circumstances and turn them for our good (Romans 8:28). He will help us deal with our problems as they arise, through His Word and Holy Spirit and sometimes through other believers. However, He does expect us to mature and to grow in discernment of good and evil (Hebrews 5:14) and to reject evil when we recognize it (1 John 1:5–10). We must remember that what a man sows shall he also reap (Galatians 6:7).

Furthermore, it's vital to realize that not all who call themselves believers are actually believers; the Bible warns of wolves dressed like sheep. "For I know this, that after my departing shall grievous wolves enter in among you, not sparing the flock" (Acts 20:29).

Today, the mentality of even many Christians is—no judgment. Divine judgment is politically incorrect, and the belief that we need no higher judge of our behavior than ourselves is a powerful element of the "new" emerging spirituality thought and practice. Without judgment, there is no need to see ourselves as sinners; there is no need for salvation, and therefore no need for the Lord Jesus Christ to die on the Cross for our sins. What's more, the panentheistic view (God is in all things) or pantheistic view (all things are God/divine) says that man is already divine; thus he does not need a Savior. Those who accept these views have no escape from sin and Satan. Without trusting in Jesus' atoning work on the Cross, they will face God's judgment without a mediator. The New Age/New Spirituality, Roman Catholicism, the emerging church, and Native American Spirituality are works-based spiritualities. Their leaders focus on what we *do* rather than on justification *by faith* through Christ, thereby taking their followers into darkness and death.

> And when they shall say unto you, Seek unto them that have familiar spirits, and unto wizards that peep, and that mutter: should not a people seek unto their God? . . . if they speak not according to this word, it is because there is no light in them. And they shall pass through it, hardly bestead and hungry: and it shall come to pass, that when they shall be hungry, they shall fret themselves, and curse their king and their God, and look upward . . . and they shall be driven to darkness. (Isaiah 8: 19-22)

For many deceivers are entered into the world, who confess not that Jesus Christ is come in the flesh. This is a deceiver and an antichrist. (2 John 1:7)

Seven

FALSE CHRISTS, PLASTIC SHAMANS, & MOTHER EARTH

A False Native American Messiah

False "Christs" exist among Native Americans just like they exist in other ethnic groups. One of the most memorable is Wovoka (born c. 1858 in Nevada), also known as Jack Wilson. Wovoka was a Paiute religious leader who combined Christianity with Paiute mysticism. He founded the Ghost Dance movement in 1890, which spread throughout much of the western United States. Wovoka saw the power Jesus wielded as magic. One biographer of Wovoka explains:

> He [Wovoka] learned about Jesus—palefaced wizard of long ago. Jesus was adept at magic. He had only to touch a man to heal him. He could change plain water into firewater. He could take one small trout, and with a hand pass, turn the trout into enough fish to feed the whole tribe. He could breathe on a dead man, and the dead man's eyes would open once again into life.[1]

Wovoka claimed to be the Messiah and told the Natives who followed him not to tell "white man" about him, saying, "Jesus is now upon the earth. He appears like a cloud. The dead are all still alive again."[2] Wovoka believed he had made a personal visit to Heaven in which he learned that:

> The enlightened ones must perform the stately circle dance in the precise manner which God and the spirits demanded. They must sing the songs the Messiah prescribed. They must wear the holy garment, which protected against danger and death. This visible badge of oneness was a shirt, marked with mystic symbols, which not only guaranteed everlasting life to the believer, but had the miraculous power to turn back even the white man's bullets.[3]

The book *Ghost Dance Messiah* states:

> To the desperate and conquered Plains tribes, in 1890, the doctrine and promises of the Paiute Messiah struck almost instant response. The Sioux, the Arapahoes, the Cheyennes, and Kiowas, in the throes of their desperation, sent investigative teams out to Nevada to sit at the feet of the Indian Jesus. The fever caught on to dozens of other tribes. Soon, across the nation, ten thousand Indians were shuffling in the Ghost Dance, and experiencing its miracles.[4]

Wovoka became the "Jesus" of his nation and of many other Native American nations. However, to truly fit the description, he needed to have been God, conceived by a virgin, sinless, holy, obedient to the Gospel, and dying a cruel death on the Cross to pay for the sins of mankind. Wovoka was nothing more than a deceived sinner and one who led many into his own deception. In the Gospel of John, it says, "In the beginning was the Word, and the Word was with God, and the Word was God." (John 1:1).

The apostle Paul knew that false teachers and false Christs would present themselves. He warned in the Book of Acts:

> For I know this, that after my departing shall grievous wolves enter in among you, not sparing the flock. Also of your own selves shall men arise, speaking perverse things, to draw away disciples after them. (Acts 20: 29-30)

Jack Wilson, "Wovoka

Paul said that through deception, our minds could become "corrupted from the simplicity that is in Christ." He warned about those who preach "another Jesus," "another spirit," and "another gospel" (2 Corinthians 11:3-4).

Satan is roaming about the earth, seeking those he may deceive. We are warned to be on the lookout for his devices:

> Be sober, be vigilant; because your adversary the devil, as a roaring lion, walketh about, seeking whom he may devour. (1 Peter 5:8)

When something (or someone) looks good or sounds good, we automatically tend to think it *is* good. The same holds true when something *feels* good. But think about how many times in the Bible we are told about spiritual deception and about those who deceive. It's one of the major themes in the Word of God. And as for false Christs (or antichrists), we are told there will be many. The prefix anti in antichrist means pseudo, another word for a counterfeit of the real thing. It may look similar and may promise the same things, but in reality, it is not the real thing. And following a counterfeit will lead one down a path to destruction at worst and deep disappointment at best. This is the very reason why we should not lean on our own understanding but acknowledge God in all our ways.

> Let no man deceive himself. If any man among you seemeth to be wise in this world, let him become a fool, that he may be wise. For the wisdom of this world is foolishness with God. For it is written, He taketh the wise in their own craftiness. (1 Corinthians 3:18–19)

SHAMANISM VS. THE TRUE CHRIST

> But refuse profane and old wives' fables, and exercise thyself rather unto godliness. (1 Timothy 4:7)

> But I [say], that the things which the Gentiles sacrifice, *they sacrifice to devils*, and not to God: and I would not that ye should have fellowship with devils. (1 Corinthians 10:20; emphasis added)

Native American Spirituality revolves around myths and visions—just like the religions of the nations surrounding Israel in ancient times. Its totems were idols, and as Paul said, when you pray to an idol, you're praying to demons. Thus, shamanism is a form of demonology.

To become a devotee of Wovoka, the Paiute false Christ, one, in effect, would be saying that Jesus Christ was a shaman. Wovoka mistook magic for the power of the Holy Spirit, much like Simon the Sorcerer did in Acts 8:9–24. He would not at all be lacking for company now, for sadly enough, a growing number of professing Christian leaders are currently promoting this same heretical view. Combining occult techniques (e.g., yoga, chanting, trance-like states, centering prayer) with Christian concepts has already become all too popular now as more and more people seek experiences through altered states of consciousness over the narrow way of truth as found in Scripture, which teaches repentance, humility, and a genuine relationship with Jesus Christ.

Shamanism refers to beliefs and practices focused on communication with the demonic spirit realm. There are many variations throughout the world, though all forms of shamanism share some basic beliefs. There are also many myths among those who practice shamanism. Take a look at some of these lies and compare these with the Word of God:

> **Lie/Myth:** The spirits can play important roles in human lives.
>
> **Truth:** The spirits are deceiving demons masquerading as helpful spirits. "Therefore it is no great thing if his [Satan's] ministers also be transformed as the ministers of righteousness" (2 Corinthians 11:15). The role of these deceiving spirits is to bring human beings into bondage, and following them is the opposite of following the Holy Spirit and living in freedom.

Lie/Myth: The shaman can control and/or cooperate with the spirits for the community's benefit as a whole.

Truth: To the contrary! The evil spirits control the shaman who is in terrible bondage. Jesus Christ does not share His kingdom with evil spirits; neither does God share His glory with another. In fact, He has reserved a place for them in Hell. And when they inhabited or possessed a person, Jesus cast them out. Read in Luke 8:26–31 about the deliverance of the demoniac who lived among the tombs and was inhabited by a legion of demons.

Lie/Myth: The spirits can be either good or bad.

Truth: ALL spirits, except the Holy Spirit, are demonic, not just some. There is no such thing as "good and bad" or "white or black" magic. It's all bad, in other words. The Holy Spirit works solely to exalt Christ. Consider the following scriptural passage:

Blessed are they that do his commandments, that they may have right to the tree of life, and may enter in through the gates into the city. For without are dogs, and sorcerers, and whoremongers, and murderers, and idolaters, and whosoever loveth and maketh a lie. (Revelation 22:14–15)

Lie/Myth: Shamans find it spiritually beneficial and essential to engage in various practices and techniques to incite trance-like states—things like singing, dancing, taking entheogens (hallucinogenic-inducing plants), meditating, and drumming.

Truth: While it is true that such practices induce trance-like states, the Bible forbids such things and strongly warns us of their spiritually defiling inherent nature. These self-induced trances invariably connect the participant to the demonic realm.

Lie/Myth: Animals play an important role, acting as omens and message-bearers, as well as representations of animal spirit guides.

Truth: Mankind was given dominion over the animals, for animals are not spiritual beings. They were not created to be worshiped or to be used for divination. In Genesis, we see:

And God said, Let us make man in our image, after our likeness: and let them have dominion over the fish of the sea, and over the fowl of the air, and over the cattle, and over all the earth, and over every creeping thing that creepeth upon the earth. (Genesis 1:26)

Lie/Myth: The shaman's spirit leaves the body and enters into the supernatural world during certain tasks.

Truth: This is an occult technique never condoned, approved, or practiced by Jesus or His disciples of the Bible. Jesus Christ never left His body nor advocated that others do so. He commands us to live by faith, trusting in Him.

But the fearful, and unbelieving, and the abominable, and murderers, and whoremongers, and sorcerers, and idolaters, and all liars, shall have their part in the lake which burneth with fire and brimstone: which is the second death. (Revelation 21:8)

Lie/Myth: The shamans can treat illnesses or sickness; they are healers.

Truth: The type of healing they manifest comes from the demonic or earthly realm, which leads only to greater bondage. Illnesses that have been cured in this manner have been known to come back with a vengeance later. "This wisdom descendeth not from above, but is earthly, sensual, devilish (James 3:15)." Although Christ used some physical means in healing, such as mud to heal sight, He never ever called on "spirit guides." Instead, we are given the following biblical approach to such matters:

> Is any sick among you? let him call for the elders of the church; and let them pray over him, anointing him with oil in the name of the Lord: And the prayer of faith shall save the sick, and the Lord shall raise him up; and if he have committed sins, they shall be forgiven him. (James 5:14-15)

While it *is* true that Jesus Christ's ministry included healing people, casting out demons, preaching the Gospel, and saving souls, the Bible clearly shows that He never sought or entered into a mystical altered state of consciousness in so doing. Instead, He humbly communed with His heavenly Father and obeyed. He did not have a sweat lodge, sing incantations, chant, dance in a frenzied manner, use the smoke of grasses, or use drums. Nor did He utilize animals as spirit guides. In fact, the Bible strictly forbids these practices.

> There shall not be found among you any one that maketh his son or his daughter to pass through the fire, or that useth divination, or an observer of times, or an enchanter, or a witch. Or a charmer, or a consulter with familiar spirits, or a wizard, or a necromancer. For all that do these things are an abomination unto the LORD: and because of these abominations the LORD thy God doth drive them out from before thee. (Deuteronomy 18:10–12)

The Lord Jesus Christ did not mend souls employing earthly, demonic means. He died on the Cross to redeem our souls in order that we should not perish in Hell for eternity. Jesus Christ was not an imposter or a hypocrite who engaged in the detestable practices performed by shamans and then turned around and sternly warned others to steer clear of these practices.

Christ says in His Word, "And if a house be divided against itself, that house cannot stand" (Mark 3:25). So, if He was a shaman, how could He have stood divided against Himself? He couldn't—which leads us back to His Word, the Bible. There He reveals Himself to all mankind as Savior, Deliverer, Redeemer, Healer, Justifier, Sanctifier, and Messiah—just to name a few. His ministry was wholly devoted to teaching about the kingdom of God so that souls could be saved. Native Spirituality lacks a Savior, Deliverer, Redeemer, Healer, Justifier, Sanctifier, and Messiah. There is an empty void in the lives of all who embrace manmade religion, and that void is very deep and dark.

Christ never taught about "Mother Earth" or practiced *earth spirituality*.[5] This is manmade teaching originating from the pit of Hell. It is found nowhere in Scripture. In fact, God says He will burn up the earth some day. In the second Book of Peter, it says:

> But the day of the Lord will come as a thief in the night; in which the heavens shall pass away with a great noise, and the elements shall melt with fervent heat, the earth also and the works that are therein shall be burned up. (2 Peter 3:10)

To reduce Jesus, the King of Kings and Lord of Lords, to an occult/mystical being and the Holy Spirit to magic is not only to deny the power of God thereof but is blasphemy and the worst form of spiritual ignorance. Jesus Christ is the very Son of God, who was born a man and died on the Cross to redeem us from our sins in order that we may have eternal life. The Holy Spirit is the "Spirit of truth" (John 14:17). What shaman ever died on the Cross for our sins? What shaman ever rose again after he died? Jesus Christ paid that penalty for us because it is impossible for a mere human being to pay it—not by works, not by doing penance, not with money, not with materials, but by the grace of God alone we are saved. Ephesians makes this very clear:

> For by grace are you saved by faith; and that not of yourselves: it is the gift of God: Not of works, lest any man should boast. (Ephesians 2:8-9)

Struggling to Maintain Their Identity

Views differ about the origins of North American Native religion, as to whether its early ancestors came from other lands or were indigenous and whether they arrived thousands of years ago or more recently. Whatever the truth, it is clear that they developed the hunting taboos, animal ceremonialism, spiritism, and shamanism that have been major elements of Native American Spirituality.

Because so many hundreds of Native religious views exist, this book limits its discussion to a general understanding of Native American Spirituality in Canada and the United States. Nevertheless, New Age or pagan spirituality has the same basic characteristics as I showed in chapter six.

Although the various tribes across North America evolved with different slants on their religious views, a basic unified view underlies them all that sees the natural world as full of supernatural meaning. Through the ceremonial rituals, practitioners seek to gain favor with the spiritual presences they believe are all around them.[6] Thus, spiritism plays a major role in their world.

In the past, the governments of the United States and Canada suppressed Native Spirituality, threatening spiritual leaders with jail sentences of up to thirty years for practicing their rituals. The Canadian government banned such Aboriginal cultural ceremonies as powwows, sweat lodges, and Indian sun dances in 1925. But such bans never worked, as they only drove these ceremonies underground. These bans were finally lifted in 1951.[7]

It took until 1978 for the U.S. to do the same with the Freedom of Religion Act. Although Canadian prisons have allowed Native sweat lodge ceremonies since the early 1980s, this has not occurred in American prisons as of yet.[8]

Today, Part I of the Canadian Charter of Rights and Freedoms says that everyone has the following fundamental freedoms:

- freedom of conscience and religion
- freedom of thought, belief, opinion, and expression, including freedom of the press and other media of communication
- freedom of peaceful assembly
- freedom of association.[9]

Thus, the Canadian Charter and the U.S. Freedom of Religion Act currently allow Native Americans the freedom to practice their spiritual traditions and preferences. These beliefs and practices are wide ranging. One source states:

> Many Native families have been devout Christians for generations. Others, particularly in the Southwest have retained their aboriginal traditions more or less intact. Most follow a personal faith that combines traditional [Native Spirituality] and Christian elements.[10]

Pan Indianism is a more recent movement, which encourages unity among the various Native groups and a return to traditional beliefs. There are even efforts to create a common Native religion.[11] Then there is the Native American Church (as mentioned in chapter six), incorporated in 1918, which claims to promote Christian beliefs and values while using peyote as a sacrament.[12]

While many Native Americans are *reawakening* to their ancient traditions, New Age and Wiccan practitioners are recognizing the occult aspects of those traditions and revising them for their own purposes. One source that advocates this blending, states:

> "Crystal skull caretakers" sit beside Native American shamans and priests, and "Star Beings," rather than buffalo, are pondered.[13]

But not all Native Americans like this trend. Some traditionalists are up in arms.

In a "Declaration of war against exploiters of Lakota Spirituality," three traditional Lakota spiritual leaders condemned:

- "...having our most precious Lakota ceremonies and spiritual practices desecrated, mocked and abused by non-Indian 'wannabes,' hucksters, cultists, commercial profiteers and self-styled 'New Age shamans' and their followers." (i.e., a hijacking of Native spirituality)
- "Having their precious Sacred Pipe sold openly at flea markets, New Age stores, etc."
- "Profit-making groups holding sweatlodges, sundances, shaminism, [*sic*] and vision quest programs for the public."
- "Inaccurate and negative portrayal of Indian people in movies and TV."
- "Efforts to create syncretistic religions by combining Native rituals and beliefs with New Age and neo-pagan spiritual paths."[14]

In 2009, an incident took place that highlighted the Native American's frustration at seeing Native Spirituality "hi-jacked" by mainstream Western society. New Age author and motivational speaker James Arthur Ray hosted a "Spiritual Warrior" retreat at Angel Valley Retreat Center near Sedona, Arizona, where one of the activities led to the deaths of three of the participants, as described in the following section.

Plastic Shamans

A *plastic shaman* is someone who basically impersonates or claims to be a shaman or a medicine man or woman, but in actuality does not have any actual cultural connection to the traditions they claim to represent:[15]

> Rather they leverage the mystique of these traditions and people's curiosity for personal gain. Generally this involves offering fake artifacts, fictional accounts in books, or illegitimate tours and ceremonies for sale.[16]

It is ironic that many "legitimate" medicine men or Native American shamans are very vocal about the dangers of plastic or fraudulent shamans. Ironic because the "pure" Native Spirituality they are trying to preserve is dangerous as well. But there is a unique danger with plastic shamans in that they often do not perform particular rituals in a "safe" manner. People have been injured and even died in miscalculated sweat lodge ceremonies. A case in point was the incident mentioned in the previous section, which took place in October 2009 with New Age guru James Ray, who had won popularity after being on the Oprah Winfrey Show. One news article described the deadly sweat lodge encounter:

> When three people died and dozens more were hospitalized from the effects of a faux Indian sweat lodge two weeks ago—during a "spiritual warrior weekend" in Sedona, Arizona, for which participants paid nearly $10,000 apiece—a harsh light was cast on the so-called New Age Movement and its greedier entrepreneurs.[17]

In 2011, Ray was sentenced to two years in prison for his role in the deaths of three people that day. Over fifty people had crammed into a four feet high sweat lodge. When many of them began vomiting, fainting, and crying out for help, Ray continued on with the ceremony.

Sometimes, these pseudo shamans incorporate nudity or sex into their mystical, New Age ceremonies, claiming this to be true Native Spirituality, when in fact this would *not* be traditional Native Spirituality. Nevertheless, today, many aspects of Native Spirituality have become commodities in our worldly culture. I have seen Native regalia, books on channeling spirit guides and beings, and shamanism sold in stores mainly promoted by the New Age Movement. Native Spirituality has become the most trendy and lucrative sector in New Age commercialism.

Many New Age practitioners are trying to reinvent shamanism in modern forms, combining its core beliefs with an eclectic assortment of philosophies and practices.

I recall Grandpa John complaining back in the late 1960s and early 1970s about such people who were into Native Spirituality. Apparently, they were allowing the media to take pictures of them while they were smudging. One Native American practitioner had this to say:

> If a person is involved in an honest smudging ceremony, that person should act and feel differently than before the ceremony. An American native should never allow smudging while people are taking pictures—N E V E R—smudging [is] a ceremony between you, the one smudging and the Creator.[18]

Grandpa John was angry because he believed that your soul can be stolen this way. He didn't realize these people were actually plastic shamans who were in the way of spiritually hijacking Native Spirituality. Such groups are still in operation today.

Some in our family believed that one of these followers of plastic shamanism had turned to Grandpa John for healing. Uncle Gil and I were seated at my grandma's kitchen table talking while Grandpa John was healing a Caucasian man from a witchcraft curse that he supposedly had received. I don't recall how, just that it apparently happened in Saskatchewan. We never expected to hear about a Caucasian going to a medicine man to be rid of a witchcraft curse. But nowadays such things seem to be happening with increasing frequency.

SHAMANS WHO FOUND JESUS

Donald Holsclaw is a former shaman. He tells of his terrifying journey into shamanism in his testimony *From Drug Addict to Shaman to Christian*. He has graciously allowed me to reprint some of his testimony in *Muddy Waters*:

"My mom and dad were not Christians and hardly ever went to church. I got into rock music early in my life, stuff like Kiss by the time I was probably twelve years old. It really took hold of my life.

. . . by my early twenties, I was doing a lot of coke and acid [LSD] and drinking very heavy. I was selling drugs to pay for my habit. I was reading *High Times* a lot. I'd read about how people could get to God through drugs; this religion was called Shamanism—that was interesting to me. . . .

"I ordered a book out of *High Times* on how to practice shamanism. I started doing the things it told to do in the book. I realized after a little while I had opened myself up to a very real and demonic world. I was having nightmares, and I could feel evil around me all the time. I was really scared.

"My mom, who wasn't a Christian at the time, said I may be eating the forbidden fruit mentioned in the Bible. . . . I decided to go get a Bible to see what it really said. I knew the devil was real by the shamanism and realized I was in deep trouble. I wanted help, and if the devil was real, God must be also.

"I realized I had been serving the devil and evil was taking me over, [and] I felt like something was trying to possess me. I kept seeing repent everywhere I read, I was so scared. I begged God to save me and change me. I begged him to help me not to be deceived, to please give me discernment, to not be deceived like that again. He changed my whole life and delivered me from Satan's power.

"My main goal in life now is to serve Him with all my heart and to expose Satan and his deceptions and to bring as many people as I can to the truth of Jesus Christ."[19]

Donald's story is but one example of the terrible bondage under which Satan desires to place people. It also shows the terrible destruction he can bring to someone's life when one dabbles in the spirit realm.

Another shaman, Shoefoot, from the Amazon Rainforest, was raised and trained to be a shaman in his tribe. At first, Shoefoot was encouraged by the help he got from the spirits, but eventually he realized there were serious problems because of the spirits. There were sicknesses among the children, vengeance being wrought upon others, abduction of women, and violent raids. The knowledge the spirits gave wasn't altogether trustworthy, which kept the tribe in a state of constant confusion and fear. In Corinthians, we are told, "For God is not the author of confusion, but of peace. (1 Corinthians 14:33).

Finally, Shoefoot grew tired of the spirits' excuses, but some of them became so violent and vicious as a result that they caused mayhem and death among his people. The drug-induced rituals where the spirits operated openly were even greater pits of insanity and violence.

Over time, Shoefoot began succumbing to feelings of abject hopelessness in trying to help his people, who consequently, were quickly deteriorating. He then tried to go even deeper into the spirit world, hoping to find more help from them. Of course, his efforts were only met with greater despair and utter futility. Somewhere during his dark spiritual journey, he became aware of a powerful Spirit "who," he was told by his spirit guides "was the enemy of his spirits and his people." An article about Shoefoot tells how he discovered the truth about this "enemy" Spirit:

> Ironically, the location where this Spirit, Yai Pada, dwelled was a beautiful place of abundance and peace, the very blessings Shoefoot desired for his tribe and for himself. Since he had been lied to so often by his spirits, he was driven to know if they were telling him the truth about Yai Pada.
>
> Fulfilling His promise given to all humanity through the prophet Jeremiah, 'And ye shall seek me, and find

> me, when ye shall search for me with all your heart' (29:13), the Lord led Shoefoot to a missionary [who] taught Shoefoot . . . that sin made us all God's enemies, yet [God] loved us so much that He sent His Son to pay the full penalty for our sins, and by admitting our sinfulness and putting our trust in Jesus and our faith in what He accomplished for us, we could have peace with the God of Peace. Moreover, he was told that all who believe in Jesus will spend eternity with Yai Pada.[20]

An account of Shoefoot's life and experiences can be read in a book titled *Spirit of the Rain Forest.* What a wonderful testimony of God's faithfulness to deliver us from darkness to light and life!

MOTHER EARTH & A GLOBAL PEACE PLAN

I include a section on Mother Earth in this chapter on false Christs because "Mother Earth" is now worshiped as a savior and a god. Even the United Nations is now debating as to whether Mother Earth "Deserves Human Rights Status"[21] as the following *Fox News* article states:

> A bloc of mostly socialist governments lead by Bolivia have put the issue on the General Assembly agenda to discuss the creation of a U.N. treaty that would grant the same rights found in the Universal Declaration of Human Rights to Mother Nature.[22]

What is significant about this is that Mother Earth may, at some point, be given the same human rights as bestowed upon a living, breathing human being. This deification of Mother Earth is animistic in nature. Earth should never be regarded as a person nor should it be worshiped as if it were a god. God did not create Mother Earth. He created a sphere for our sustenance and for His glory. Yet, the Bible warns this will happen in the last days before Christ's return:

> Who changed the truth of God into a lie, and worshipped and served the creature more than the Creator. (Romans 1:25)

The U.N. is romanticizing Mother Earth in the name of political correctness and global salvation. This peace plan process will eventually set up the religion of the Antichrist. The U.N.'s peace plan includes global political cooperation, global economic cooperation, and global spiritual cooperation (i.e., the three-legged stool).

At the 2010 G8 World Religions Summit, researcher, and writer Carl Teichrib observed:

> A sacred fire was lit. Mother Earth, we were told, needs to hear that we love her, so give a "prayer of gratitude" to the Earth; "Because out of Mother Earth comes all we need to live . . . she gives us the food, the water, the medicines, and the teachings."
>
> We were asked to privately perform a water ritual, for this will give strength to Mother Earth. Everything that's alive, "even the water" it was explained to the delegates and observers, has the spirit. We were told that religiously speaking, "there is not only one way, there [are] many ways"—and to go to the sacred fire and "invoke the spirits."
>
> Drummers summoned the power of the eagle spirit, because it brings "the spirit of love, it brings vision. The Eagle carries our wishes and our prayers." And this eagle spirit will tell the Great Spirit of the wonderful things happening in this gathering.[23]

Teichrib said that attendees were welcomed as "religious equals" and that it was important that we "offer our service, and ourselves, and our lives" to the "God we know by so many names."[24]

This is all part of a counterfeit world peace plan that is falling into place very quickly. Most people (and even most professing

Christians) are totally unaware that a global peace plan and a one-world religion are already well in hand and being spear-headed by a select "collective" of world leaders. Within the Christian church, men like Rick Warren, author of *The Purpose Driven Life*, are helping to expedite this world-wide peace plan.[25]

Canadian author Roger Oakland discusses Rick Warren's peace plan in *Faith Undone,* his book dealing with the emerging church. Oakland says:

> Rick Warren has an ambitious plan called the P. E. A. C. E. Plan, which he hopes will usher in the kingdom of God here on earth. . . . Warren believes he has uncovered the missing component for success—an *all-inclusive* church. . . . This inclusive church is the third leg of what Warren calls a "three-legged stool. . . ." Part of Warren's process is for the church to lay down its differences with other religions and secular entities so that a more powerful and effective body can be developed. . . . By saying "you don't have to change your beliefs," Warren is able to stretch the boundaries of his global peace plan to include virtually every belief system and persuasion. This would be the religious (spiritual) leg of the three-legged stool.[26]

Whether it is the U.N.'s Mother Earth plan, Native Spirituality's earth and nature worshiping, or Rick Warren's three-legged stool peace plan, all originate from the same source of "wisdom" as put forth in James:

> This wisdom descendeth not from above, but is earthly, sensual, devilish. (James 3:15)

The most devastating aspect of this earth-based (Mother Earth) spirituality, however, is that it is the very antithesis of an earth or world fashioned, created, and spoken into existence by a loving Creator. Earth, a finite ball of dirt, gases, inert elements, and minerals can never love us, nurture us, and redeem us. Yet God, the Creator of all things, can do all these things for us and satisfy our souls, if we allow Him into our hearts. It seems like such an obvious choice, yet so many don't see it.

NAMES OF SOME NORTH AMERICAN INDIAN GODS:

Kitchi Manitou—The "Supreme Being" who created and filled the universe with life force. He is therefore highly respected by his followers and owns everything in the Universe but is just as happy to allow humanity to play with some of it.

In return for his kindness, Kitchi Manitou is treated with the greatest of respect—individual ritual offerings of smoke extending from a sacred pipe, which then carries prayers to the heavens where Kitchi Manitou lives.

Manitou—Often confused with Kitchi Manitou, Manitou is the god that gives its all-embracing spirit power to animals, plants and rock. We can see that inanimate objects are given life by this Manitou. The word "Manitou" is usually translated "spirit."

Nokomis—A goddess, also known as Mother Earth, who is the swinging grandmother of all Earth Mothers. A female deity.

Weetikoo—A cannibal and a terrifying god with a never-ending hunger for flesh and blood.

We can see from the names of the North American gods and their characteristics that they are not one and the same like the True God of the Bible is, despite the many names ascribed to Him.

SOME HEBREW NAMES OF THE GOD OF THE BIBLE:

ADONAI—Lord and Master (Genesis 15:2)

EL-ECHAD—The One God (Malachi 2:10)

ELOHIM—God, Judge, Creator (Genesis 1:1, Psalm 29:1)

EL-ELYON—The Most High God (Isaiah 14:13-14)

EL-ROI—The God Who Sees (Genesis 16:13)

EL-SHADDAI—Lord God Almighty (Genesis 48:3)

JEHOVAH-RAAH—The Lord, my Shepherd (Psalm 23:1)

JEHOVAH-SHAMMAH—The Lord is There (present) (Ezekiel 48:35)

JEHOVAH-RAPHA—The Lord that Heals (Exodus 15:26)

JEHOVAH-JIREH—The Lord will Provide (Genesis 22:13-14)

JEHOVAH-NISSI—The Lord, my Banner (Exodus 17:15)

JEHOVAH-SHALOM—The Lord is Peace (Judges 6:24)

For a more complete list of names of the God of the Bible, see Appendix II at the back of this book.

The lists above with the names of the God of the Bible and the gods of Native Spirituality are by no means exhaustive lists, but they are comprehensive enough to enable one to readily see the differences between the God of the Bible and the lesser gods or fallen angels and demons. The true God of the Bible says this about all other gods and unbelievers:

> I am the LORD, and there is none else, there is no God beside me: I girded thee, though thou hast not known me. (Isaiah 45:5)

USING TRAGEDY FOR CATALYSTS OF CHANGE

Many Native Spiritual practitioners today are encouraging people to use tragedies as catalysts for change (i.e., a return to Native Spirituality). In other words, they are telling Native American's to "return" to their Native Spirituality roots as a response to the atrocities and tragedies that have happened in their lives (such as in the residential schools). But a return to such "roots" only compounds the problems, which lead to further descent into utter deception and darkness.

My late Grandpa John and Uncle Sam used tragedies such as suicides and murder to call their people to return to Native Spirituality.

In one article titled "Manitoba's Native leaders see a return to ancient traditions and spiritual values as the solution to modern problems" it stated that First Nations elders in Winnipeg, Manitoba (where it is said that 10 percent of the population is aboriginal) "see a return to the old traditions and Native Spirituality as key to overcoming [the] challenges" of alcoholism, poverty, and crime among native people.[27]

How sad to see that Native leaders will draw already grieving people further into grief and darkness through empty philosophies and manmade traditions. We have deceived ourselves for so long by our own beliefs in Native Spirituality and/or Roman Catholicism, which, in turn, left us vulnerable to more deception due to the blindness already at work in each of us. Is it not time we finally move forward and open ourselves to seeking God's truth and the truth about these false teachings passed on down to us multi-generationally? We at least owe ourselves this much.

So, think about what exactly the Native Spirituality practitioners are really proposing when God strongly warns us against engaging in the following as put forth in Deuteronomy 18:9-12:

AUGURY: Omen foretelling.

WIZARDRY: The art or practice of magic.

SOOTHSAYING: Fortune-telling and oracle interpretation.

DIVINATION: Uncovering hidden knowledge via occult or supernatural means.

CHARMERS: Like an enchanter or one who uses magic or sorcery to put someone or something under a spell.

NECROMANCY: Witchcraft, sorcery, or black magic in general; the practice of communicating with the dead.

SORCERY: Witchcraft, black (and white) magic. Also, the art, practices, or spells of a person who channels or wields supernatural powers via the aid of evil spirits.

MEDIUMS: Intermediary human channels of communication; a person who conveys spiritual messages; an intervening substance through which something is conveyed, transmitted or carried on; a person thought to have the power to communicate with the spirits of the dead or with agents of another world or dimension (also called "psychic").[28]

And, last but not least—making a son or daughter pass through fire (e.g., child sacrifice to the god of Molech). God also has this to say:

> When thou art come into the land which the LORD thy God giveth thee, thou shalt not learn to do after the abominations of those nations. . . . For all that do these things are an abomination unto the LORD: and because of these abominations the LORD thy God doth drive them out from before thee. (Deuteronomy 18: 9, 12)

This should be enough to get everyone's attention and make us sit up and take note. Yet, people continue to follow false teachers headlong down the broad path of eternal damnation. What kind of love is this, that it should love people down a slippery slope straight into the pit of Hell itself? I don't say they do it deliberately, for Native Spiritual practitioners fail to see God's truth because the "god of this world" has blinded their eyes for one purpose—so that the "light of the glorious gospel of Christ, who is the image of God" will not shine in their lives (2 Corinthians 4:4), and they will spend eternity separated from God.

The real catalyst for change that should be used universally is being made aware of the wretchedness of our sinful nature so we might be cut to the quick and turn to the Lord Jesus Christ for forgiveness. Then true change and freedom from sin, bondage, and oppression can occur in our lives through our newfound belief and repentance. Countless numbers of native and non-native people alike are given over to substance abuse of one form or another and/or are sadly caught in a web of lies.

Though not well documented, it is well known in Native communities that there are two real reasons why many of our people wind up on Skid Row—residential schools and Native Spirituality. The lingering effects of the atrocities suffered in residential schools and the bondages and oppression resulting from engaging in Native Spirituality or witchcraft leaves many natives looking like holocaust victims from substance abuse they have been involved in to compensate for the pain and tragedies in their lives and the memories from their childhoods. And yet, as I mentioned earlier, they are encouraged by professing Christian native leaders to use these tragedies as catalysts for change to return to Native Spirituality.

Again, this is found nowhere in Scripture! I came from this background and know what set me free from these lies. It was only through Jesus Christ's forgiveness of my own sins that I was finally free at last. And upon receiving Him by faith through His grace, He came into my heart, and I have had fellowship with Him ever since. As new believers, we are promised in the Gospel of John:

> And ye shall know the truth, and the truth shall make you free. (John 8:32)

EIGHT

NATIVE SPIRITUALITY "RENEWAL" EMERGES

Watch ye therefore, and pray always, that ye may be accounted worthy to escape all these things that shall come to pass, and to stand before the Son of man. (Luke 21:36)

While those practicing Native Spirituality may believe they are practicing a completely unique form of spirituality, originating with them, they couldn't be further from the truth. Native Spirituality is just one part of a vast movement that is creating a paradigm shift in our present-day culture away from biblical Christianity and replacing it with an all-inclusive interspiritual global religion that relies heavily upon mystical practices. The results will create a "Christianity" that has no resemblance to biblical Christianity whatsoever.

As part of this massive global shift, many Native American or First Nations tribes are exploring the renewal of their ancient spiritual traditions and reinstituting ancestral and mystical practices. Natives involving themselves in this pursuit see this as an opportunity to bring recognition to the forgotten and once persecuted Native American religion. They fail to realize that they are actually participating in a mass deception spreading throughout the world in the days prior to Christ's return.

One example of this "awakening" among Native Americans

took place on July 30th, 2007, when the Lummi Nation in Washington State sponsored the Paddle to Lummi Canoe Journey 2007 for six days. Its motto was Traveling the Traditional Highways of Our Ancestors, and its theme was Xwialken etse Tl'aneq—Lummi for the Return of the Potlatch.[1]

Salish canoe families from around the Northwest Coast gathered to celebrate their first potlatch since 1937. Potlatches, a distinctive tradition in the area, focused on stabilizing relationships among tribes, feasting, celebrating, and giving gifts. The call was to celebrate "as the Lummi Nation Reawakens, Renews and Revives their ancient traditions."[2]

Many other examples exist, as well, that show how this spiritual "renewal" is taking place within the lives of Native Americans and First Nations people. Richard Twiss, of the Lakota Sioux tribe, is looking for this renewal or awakening among Native people. In his book, *One Church, Many Tribes*, Twiss states:

> This is a time of transition in ministry among indigenous believers around the world—a time of exploration and sincere inquiring of the Lord for *new perspectives* and *approaches* to Native ministry. Around the globe among indigenous Christians, cultural identity is surfacing as the key dynamic in *this emerging new Native ministry paradigm* and *spiritual awakening.*[3] (emphasis added)

Twiss adds:

> Christians are debating the use of Native American drums, gourds, rattles and dances as legitimate expressions of godly faith. In the next decade or so, this controversy will also subside and we will hear and see indigenous sounds and movements in church services across the land in glorious worship to Jesus Christ. Indeed, *that day is already dawning.*[4] (emphasis added)

What Twiss is saying is very scary because a lot of people will be deceived into thinking that what he is proposing is a good thing. But while many Native American Christians, like Twiss, are looking for a great spiritual awakening within the First Nations and Native American groups—primarily by incorporating Native Spirituality cultural practices into their Christianity—right under their noses, a massive worldwide deception authored by Satan is incorporating Native Spirituality into its plan and is surging forward, ultimately forsaking the purity of the Gospel message.

NATIVE SPIRITUALITY INCORPORATED INTO SOCIETY

While Native Spirituality is being introduced into the lives of countless Native people, at the same time, Native Spirituality is being incorporated into contemporary culture: in popular forms of interspirituality such as goddess worship[5] in public schools where teachers are requiring their classes to study Native religion as part of multiculturalism; throughout the environmental movement;[6] and in the work of prominent politicians such as former Vice President Al Gore.[7] Even the movies *Pocahontas* and *Dances With Wolves* have given mainstream culture a "crash course in Native spirituality."[8] Partly in overcompensation for very real injustices committed against Native Americans, Native Spirituality has become politically correct inasmuch as traditional biblical Christianity is on a fast track to becoming politically *incorrect*. Sadly, in the process, the Gospel which is "the power of God unto salvation" (Romans 1:16) is being pushed aside, as if it were to blame—leaving countless numbers of people—both Native American and non-Native—without the sure hope that only comes through knowing Christ.

NATIVE SPIRITUALITY AND THE CATHOLIC CHURCH—"A NATURAL FIT"

The Catholic Church has joined the ranks of those embracing Native Spirituality. In a November 2006 article by *Western Catholic Reporter* titled "Catholic School Makes Room For Native

Spirituality," the principal of Ben Calf Robe Catholic School in Alberta states that the school, made up of 200 native children, "combines the teaching and Gospels of the Catholic Church with the various aspects of native spirituality."[9] The article states:

> There are four sacred drums in the school and some 60 drummers. Drumming is the sacred heart beat of Mother Earth, Richardson said. "When the drum is beat upon, we believe that all of the prayers within the children are lifted to God." . . . In their monthly liturgical celebrations, the school uses the Catholic rite but they bring in native spirituality in the methods of smudging and the prayers to the Creator.[10]

The principal of Ben Calf Robe Catholic School says that the "similarities between Catholicism and native traditions and processes are evident."[11] He adds:

> [W]e believe Catholicism and native spirituality are equal . . . We don't see one being more important and we don't see them being entwined. We do see them over-lapping at times.[12]

In another article "Native Spirituality Celebrated in Catholic School System," a Native Studies teacher in the Canadian Catholic school system "is very serious about joining two strands of his Métis heritage—Catholicism and Native spirituality—something he sees as a natural fit."[13] This resonance between Native Spirituality and Catholicism isn't strictly limited to Canada either. It's happening in the United States too. In an article in the *News of the Northwest Jesuits,* a Montana Jesuit novice says he has found "a beautiful marriage between Catholic and Native Spirituality," and is encountering "new light" in the sweat lodge.[14] The article describes what transpires in a sweat lodge ceremony:

> The space eventually is packed with Nakoda and White

> Clay tribe members of every age, surrounding the awestruck Jesuit guest. Three young men bring rocks from the blazing fire outside and drop them into a pit. The holy man—whom Herman describes as entirely Indian and entirely Catholic—douses his flashlight and begins splashing water and tossing sweet grass on the smoldering stones. Red sparks dance, intermittently lighting up the many Native faces. The people chant sacred songs in their native language, calling on their local saints, the ancestors.[15]

Native Spirituality Embraced by Mainstream Christianity

Within the evangelical/Protestant church, Native Spirituality is cropping up more and more all the time. For instance, the Mennonite Church Canada offers on their Resource Centre website a Medicine Wheel Poster. It states:

> This poster is a tool for living in harmony with God, each other and creation.
>
> It's a part of the Reaching Up to God our Creator resource box which highlights the common ground of Aboriginal Sacred Teachings and the Bible, in the hope of fostering respect and understanding among Aboriginal and non-Aboriginal communities.[16]

Also on the Mennonite Church Canada website is a booklet titled *Teachings of the Sacred Tree* "to compare Aboriginal Sacred Teachings about the Sacred Tree and the Bible's use of trees."[17] The site also offers several resources by Native American Richard Twiss, a leader in the Indigenous People's Movement (IPM), as well as several other resources on Native Spirituality, the emerging church, and contemplative mysticism.

The ELCA (Evangelical Lutheran Church in America) is another Protestant denomination that is embracing Native

Spirituality. In *Lutheran Woman Today* magazine, the president of a Lutheran seminary wrote this in an article titled "Dream Catchers: The ELCA Commission for Women":

> Beside the bed of my now-teenage daughter hangs a dream catcher, one of the many treasures of Native American culture. According to legend, the dream catcher filters dreams, sending good ones to the sleeper and trapping bad ones until they evaporate at dawn's first light.
>
> I thank God for the past 15 years of history during which the Commission for Women of the Evangelical Lutheran Church in America has been a dream catcher for thousands upon thousands in our church and beyond.[18]

You can find examples all over the Internet of mainstream Christian groups and denominations that are integrating Native Spirituality. Medicine wheels, circles, dream catchers, sweat lodges, and shamanism—it's all there.

In 2011, a book titled *The Circle Maker: Praying Circles Around Your Biggest Dreams and Greatest Fears* by emerging church pastor, Mark Batterson, was released. Batterson says his book is inspired by a legendary Jewish sage, Honi, the Circle-Drawer. The premise behind the book is that if we draw circles around important things in our lives, including our prayers, we will receive great blessings. In the legend of Honi in 1 BC, the land was subjected to a drought. In the excerpt below, Batterson says:

> With a six-foot staff in his hand, Honi began to turn like a math compass. His circular movement was rhythmical and methodical. Ninety degrees. One hundred and eighty degrees. Two hundred and seventy degrees. Three hundred and sixty degrees. He never looked up as the crowd looked on. After what seemed like hours, but had only been seconds, Honi stood inside the circle he had drawn.[19]

Sure enough, it rained, and Batterson went on to say, "The circle he drew in the sand became a sacred symbol."[20] Whether God brought rain in answer to Honi's prayers or not, I will not try to speculate, but what Batterson has done in his book is turn "circle making" into a practice and a ritual (based on drawing circles) that will supposedly bring great results in a person's life.

While Batterson doesn't talk about Native Spirituality in his book, I feel it is worth mentioning his book and his "circle making" because this is a way that conditions Christians to more readily accept Native Spirituality, whether Batterson intended it or not. Everything in Native Spirituality is done in circles because the power of the world works in circles, so everything is deemed circular from childhood to worship. As the moon, sun, and earth are all round, so it is that all circles attract a spiritual energy as does symbolic expression. The circle that the medicine wheel represents is an integration of energy and matter, as well as spirit and man, so as to achieve a greater spiritual understanding and creation. Some segments of Native Spirituality involving circles are: round dances, talking circles, pipe ceremonies, drums, four quadrants (north, south, east and west), seasons, and life of man.

THE EMERGING CHURCH, THE NEW AGE, AND NATIVE SPIRITUALITY

The emerging church is a movement that is said to be a new way to do Christianity, a way that is supposed to reach out to the postmodern generation in a more relevant way than traditional Christianity. In reality, the emerging church, which is really a *merging* church, is a full-scale ecumenical effort to unite all religions against biblical Christianity by using mystical practices to accomplish this. In the emerging church, doctrine becomes unimportant while unity at all costs becomes the most important thing.

Richard Twiss talks about "heal[ing] the rifts"[21] between Natives and Anglo-Saxons, Democrats and Republicans, men and women, rich and poor, etc. and asserts how we can "all have a part to play in the healing of our nation [America]."[22] This is exactly what the emerging church is proposing to do. But the healing of the nations (America, Canada, or any part of the world) is not going to happen before Jesus Christ returns. The teaching that we can, in and of ourselves, usher in the Kingdom of God on earth now before His return is heretical. Our focus, as Native or non-Native Christians, needs to be the preaching of the Gospel according to the Holy Scriptures. It is not the earth we are to save but rather men, women, and children's souls.

When Twiss tells us to "imagine Native believers enjoying the fragrant aroma of burning sage, sweet grass or cedar"[23] or "smudging,[24] I believe he is misleading many. Galatians 3:28 tells us, "There is neither Jew nor Greek, there is neither bond nor free, there is neither male nor female: for ye are all one in Christ Jesus." In other words, our focus as born-again believers isn't to practice rituals from the cultures we were born into. We are born again, into a brand new culture—God's culture. The one "culture" that God has bestowed on all mankind is the Gospel; it is the one heritage passed on to us by God, yet we are destroying it today.

> Therefore if any man be in Christ, he is a new creature: old things are passed away; behold, all things are become new. (2 Corinthians 5:17)

In 2010 at the Emergent Village Theological Conference, Richard Twiss was part of this emerging church event. A blog for the event states:

> Richard Twiss . . . began by blessing us with sage incense and having a member of his team dance a healing dance. . . . He moved from rejecting his reservation upbringing, to re-discovering his heritage and hating white people, coming to faith in Christ through evangelical churches, walking away again from his heritage, to re-re-discovering his Native culture and integrating it into his faith.[25]

The emerging church fits in very well with Native Spirituality and Catholicism. Icons, incense, earth-based spirituality, ushering in the kingdom of God, and healing for the earth through ecumenical unity, mantras and chanting—these are all elements they have in common with each other.

In *One Church, Many Tribes*, Richard Twiss echoes Rob Bell, a leader in the emerging church. Twiss talks about removing the barriers between the "sacred" and the "secular."[26] He says that "Native people do not have a split view of reality."[27] On Bell's national tour, Everything is Spiritual,[28] Bell tells his audiences that God is in everything and no gap exists between the secular and the spiritual. Twiss says that "Western Christians struggle with . . . a dualistic belief"[29] with regard to the secular and the spiritual. Whether Twiss realizes it or not, he is describing a core viewpoint in the New Age and occultism where the secular (the flesh or carnal man) and the spiritual (God) are one. I think this explanation by Christian author Ray Yungen demonstrates the subtleties that lie within *bridging the gap* between the secular and the spiritual (i.e., man and God) in his book *A Time of Departing*:

> Satan is not simply trying to draw people to the dark side of a good versus evil conflict. Actually, he is trying to eradicate the gap between himself and God, between good and evil, altogether. When we understand this approach it helps us see why . . . Jack Canfield said he felt God flowing through *all* things. . . . Such reasoning implies that God has given His glory to all of creation; since Satan is part of creation, then he too shares in this glory, and thus is "*like the Most High*." . . .
>
> If the all-is-one view were true, then salvation through a Redeemer would become unnecessary and Jesus' death on the Cross would be rendered altogether futile and pointless. In order for the Cross to make *any* sense, there must be a separation between God's perfect nature and Man's sin nature.[30]

The Native view, which maintains there is no division between the secular and the spiritual, goes against what the Bible says about the wretched carnality of man. God is so holy and so pure that He cannot even look upon such sinfulness. It is only through the perfection, sinlessness, and the sacrifice of Jesus Christ, His only begotten Son, and through being washed clean by His blood that anyone can be saved.

There *is* a gap between the sacred and the secular, and there *is* only One mediator Who can rectify that. Native Spirituality, Catholicism, and the New Age—none of these belief systems can do it nor can they eradicate that huge chasm that has been fixed between God and man. This may be hard for us to understand because the Bible also says "God so loved the world . . ." and is "not willing that any should perish" (John 3:16 and 2 Peter 3:9). But yet, by the same token, John 3:16 also makes it very clear that only "whosoever believeth on Him will not perish but will have everlasting life." He has bestowed upon every man and woman the ability to believe upon Him in as great a measure as He has also given every man the ability to reject Him. Thus, we are all without excuse.

The plan of the emerging church is to see the earth "healed" by bringing in a global, all-inclusive kingdom of God that would include all religions and all people. The problem with an all-inclusive "kingdom" is that there is no room for a Savior who proclaims there is only one way to Heaven. One very popular New Age/New Spirituality proponent who believes man is on the threshold of enlightenment and healing for the earth says this:

> It will take an unprecedented act of courage, on a grand scale. You may have to do something virtually unknown in the annals of human history. . . . You may have to give up some of your most sacred beliefs. . . . let me make something clear. *The era of the Single Savior is over.* What is needed now is joint action, combined effort, collective co-creation.[31] (emphasis added)

How is the world going to grab hold of this "collective" effort to unite together and save the world? Through mysticism and occult practices. And because mysticism is such a major component in Native Spirituality, the emerging church, and the New Age, it is easy to see how these three spiritualities are really on the same path. And it is a path that excludes the single Savior of the world.

BIBLICAL NATIVE AMERICANS

There *are* Native American Christians who are taking a stand for the biblical Gospel. In their Preamble to "A Biblical Position by Native Leaders on Native Spirituality," Indian Bible College in Arizona states:

> One of the most critical issues facing the Native Christian Church today is the effort to revive, adapt and utilize Native cultural forms in worship of the church. In the light of the resurgence of Native religious traditionalism, the coming of the peyote movement (Native American Church), the influx of New Age philosophy, and questions concerning Native spirituality and biblical truth, we as Native believers in Christ . . . have gathered together to speak with one voice on these subjects to the body of Christ at large, basing our responses on the clear statements of the revealed Word of God.[32]

They define this mixture as syncretism, stating:

> By syncretism, we refer specifically to the subtle attempt to integrate biblical truth and faith in Christ with non-biblical Native religious beliefs, practices, and forms. The result is an adulteration of biblical truth and the birth of "another gospel. (Galatians 1:6-9)[33]

The Oujé-Bougoumou Cree tribe, a large Christian community, is another example of Native American Christians who are not caving into the Native Spirituality renewal. In 2010, the

Oujé-Bougoumou voted to dismantle a sweat lodge that had been constructed. The resolution to get rid of the sweat lodge stated:

> The practice of the sweat lodge and its rituals are not restricted to merely medical [pursuit] of healing, but [are] in essence a way to contact and communicate with the spirit world through shamanism.[34]

The resolution stated that "the Cree community's elders did not want any form of 'Native spirituality or practices' in Ouje-Bougoumou."[35] The Cree community received much criticism for their resolution, and a number of media sources wrote negative stories about what happened, suggesting that the resolution would result in nothing but strife and division. In fact, while there are countless negative references of the incident on the Internet, I couldn't find one site or source that commended the Oujé-Bougoumou. This book may very well prove to be the only place where these believers *are* commended. I see them as being obedient and faithful to God's Word; and their courage and integrity with regard to truth should set an example for other believers to follow. But it certainly wasn't a politically correct thing to do. Sadly enough, many professing Christians, both Native and non-Native, do not understand shamanism and the grave ramifications of embracing occultism. If they did, they would rejoice over the sweat lodge being torn down. But instead, many look upon it as being restrictive, limiting, injurious, and counterproductive to the cause inspired by an "awakening" in Native Americans to return to their religious roots.

These are perilous times for all Bible-believing Christians. Jesus said that if we follow Him, the world will hate us, and we will suffer persecution. Many have gone before us who have paid dearly with their very lives. May God give us that kind of faith.

> If ye were of the world, the world would love his own: but because ye are not of the world, but I have chosen you out of the world, therefore the world hateth you. (John 15:19)

NINE

CAN CULTURES BE REDEEMED?

> [Indigenous People's Movement] leaders teach that God has been redeeming cultures and that He placed in all cultures a way for men to have a relationship with God outside of the Gospel.[1]

DID GOD CREATE CULTURES?

A growing trend in the evangelical church is what is referred to as "redeeming the cultures" or "Cultural Identification." Essentially, it is the idea that God created cultures and has no desire for anyone to leave their cultural practices but can incorporate their belief in Jesus into their already existing culture. Mike Oppenheimer of Let Us Reason Ministries has studied this "redeeming the culture" movement extensively and writes:

> The new idea being presented is that God has left certain elements in every culture that are redeemable qualities, pathways to Himself . . . that He revealed Himself to nearly all indigenous people groups *prior to the Gospel* being brought to them [and that] in every culture "God has left treasures and worthy traditions within the indigenous cultures" [and that] we can bring Jesus Christ to people and then leave them to worship God in their own cultural and religious ways. . . .

> What is taught is that God set forth His plan of salvation through all ancient cultures and that "redemptive analogies" can be found in most, if not all, cultures.[2]

But *did* God really create cultures? I do not believe He did because cultures are man-made. *Webster's Dictionary* defines culture as being: "the customary beliefs, social forms, and material traits of a racial, religious, or social group." Another definition states:

> The quality in a person, or society that rises from interest in arts, letters, scholarly pursuits, etc. 2. a particular form or state of civilization.[3]

On the contrary to what leaders in the "redeeming the cultures" movement teach, most cultures were "pagan, polytheistic and animistic."[4] For most of these cultures, there was a significant emphasis placed on religious practices. Oppenheimer points out that the words culture or society cannot be found in the Bible, but rather it talks about "nations" and how these nations worshiped false gods as opposed to the "one true God"[5] (read Romans 1).

What does the Bible have to say about the different nations (cultures)? In Deuteronomy, we are cautioned to:

> Take heed to yourself that you are not ensnared to follow them . . . that you do not inquire after their gods, saying, 'How did these nations serve their gods? I also will do likewise.' You shall not worship the LORD your God in that way; for every abomination to the LORD which He hates they have done to their gods. (Deuteronomy 12:30-32)

And Deuteronomy 18:14 tells us not to "follow the abominations of those nations."

In all of human history, God has sanctioned just one culture, and that was Israel. This may be a humbling thing for other cultures to accept, but this is what the Word of God clearly demonstrates as the prophet Isaiah said, "I will place salvation in Zion for Israel my glory" (Isaiah 46:13). Then, after Jesus came and died upon the Cross, people from every other culture were given the opportunity to accept God's free gift of salvation through Jesus Christ. The Bible says that we can be grafted in as adopted sons and daughters. And God takes the born-again, grafted-in believer and separates him or her from the world to Himself "to take out of them a people for his name" (Acts 15:14).

Also in Acts, Barnabas and Paul cried out to the Gentiles, who were about to offer sacrifice to them, saying:

> [W]ho in bygone generations allowed all nations to walk *in their own ways.* (Acts 14:16, emphasis added)

Paul and Barnabas said this because they were shocked by the ignorance and blasphemous behavior of the people.

The apostle Peter reminds us that God has set apart "a chosen generation, a royal priesthood, an holy nation, a peculiar people" so that we who believe on Him would be called "out of darkness into his marvellous light" (1 Peter 2:6-10). God calls people out of their cultures and invites them to come into His kingdom.

Can We Redeem the Cultures?

In the Gospel of Matthew, it says:

> Go ye therefore, and teach all nations, baptizing them in the name of the Father, and of the Son, and of the Holy Ghost: Teaching them to observe all things whatsoever I have commanded you. (Matthew 28:19-20)

We are to go and preach to the different cultures and teach them "to observe all things" that God has instructed in the Word of God. Nowhere in Scripture does it even remotely suggest that one's culture is to be redeemed. And yet, there are leaders within

Christianity who are teaching this very thing. In a YWAM training manual, it states:

> Appreciating one's culture is appreciating the creation of God in a unique and beautiful manner. As disciples of Jesus Christ we are also called to redeem our culture as we grow in God.[6]

Within the Indigenous People's Movement, leaders are teaching that each culture already had God's truth before they ever heard the Gospel. Leon Siu, a leader of this movement, states:

> A few years ago some friends and I were contemplating how we would be able to reach indigenous peoples and we thought that what was prevalent at that time was a misconception among, within the church of God's presence here in the islands. The misconception that, as was expressed earlier, was that God didn't arrive until the missionaries arrived. You know, and so when we started to look at this we started to look into our culture and see what things within our culture what God had originally intended for this particular group of people, Hawaiians.[7]

But Scripture tells us that the Gospel was kept a "mystery" hidden "from ages and from generations, but now is made manifest to his saints" (Colossians 1:25-26). This is why Jesus gave that command to the disciples to go to all the nations sharing the truth of God's Word. The people of the world's cultures did not have that truth until it was brought to them.

On Leon Siu's ministry website, it states that they want to show "indigenous people, missionaries and Christians . . . the true nature of Jesus," saying that His way is not to be a "foreign religion that destroys people groups and their cultures, but one that brings people groups and their cultures to their highest fulfillment."[8]

Sandy Simpson, founder of Deception in the Church ministry in Hawaii, has written an expose titled "Reasons to Reject the

'World Christian Gathering on Indigenous People' Movement." He tells readers:

> In the Old Testament God revealed Himself to the Jews exclusively and there was no salvation apart from the Jews. In the New Testament God revealed Himself through the apostles, and especially through Paul to the Gentiles. All the gods of the nations were and are false gods (Deuteronomy 32:17; 1 Corinthians 10:20, Jeremiah 16:19, Amos 2:4).
>
> Even the "supreme beings" of the nations are not God, as in the case of Amen (Amon) of Egypt (Jeremiah 46:25), Hadad of the Arameans (1 Kings 20:28), Marduk of Babylon (Daniel 3:16-18) and many other "detestable" gods.[9]

Another research ministry, Discernment Research Group, warns that "the new heresies teach that man can come to Christ without the Gospel of Salvation but by some other avenue inherent in their culture and religion." DRG describes what this view is really like:

> And they don't need Jesus to be saved, but can call upon their own local deity. And once they get "saved," they can "redeem" the pagan religious practices in their culture and make it part of their new faith. They never need to separate from their old ways. In fact, they are encouraged to bring back the old pagan ways![10]

We cannot call on strange gods and find salvation. The Bible is absolutely clear about this:

> Hear, O my people . . . if thou wilt hearken unto me; There shall no strange god be in thee; neither shalt thou worship any strange god. (Isaiah 81:8-9)

This "progressive" way of looking at evangelism is prevalent and widespread now. One of its key leaders, Daniel Kikawa, author of *Perpetuated in Righteousness,* believes that:

> Christians should cease representing Jesus as the Son of the foreign God of a foreign people. . . . We should instead *introduce Jesus* as the Son of *their* creator God.[11] (emphasis added)

John Dawson, president of YWAM, would agree with what Kikawa says. He states that Kikawa's book "points the way to an exciting new understanding" of the Gospel.[12]

But this "new understanding" is very flawed. You can't just add Jesus to any religion or cultural belief system and say that is the biblical Gospel. The Bible says, "strait is the gate, and narrow is the way, which leadeth unto life" (Matthew 7:14). In man's carnal mind, he cannot accept this. But when we learn to trust in Jesus Christ as our Lord and Savior, and when we come to believe the Bible is the inerrant Word of God, then we can rejoice that He has provided a way of escape from eternal damnation. He has not left us alone. We no longer complain or lament that there is only *one* way to Heaven—rather, we rejoice that there *IS* a way to Heaven. It is like this little analogy: A woman is in a house caught on fire, and there is no way to get out. Suddenly, in through the door bursts a big strong firefighter. "Ma'am, I am here to rescue you." Will she say, "Are you the *ONLY* way out?" No, she will rejoice that there *IS* a way out. That is how God earnestly, zealously, and jealously longs to have it be with us.

> For I am not ashamed of the gospel of Christ: for it is the power of God unto salvation to every one that believeth; to the Jew first, and also to the Greek. (Romans 1:16)

The following comparison chart shows the differences between man's view and God's view of cultures:[13]

Man's View: All cultures are equal in their worth.

God's View: All cultures are not equal.

Man's View: God loves all cultures and nations as they are.

God's View: God does love all people but not their cultures. He does not accept their various ways to worship but has given man the correct manner in which to worship.

Man's View: All religious practices and rituals are acceptable ways to approach God.

God's View: Only one way is given by God that is acceptable, through Jesus Christ, His only begotten Son.

Man's View: We are all united as one humanity and should accept everyone as they are.

God's View: Our humanity is united in sin (in Adam), resulting in our separation from God, and we need to be united in Christ. Christ, and Christ alone, then becomes our common denominator.

Man's View: All the gods of the nations are the same or have insignificant differences.

God's View: The gods of the nations are false; YHWH alone is God, and there is no other according to His own Word.

Ephesians tells us that before we heard the Gospel of Jesus Christ, we were without hope. We cannot obtain this hope through the gods of the nation's cultures.

> Wherefore remember, that ye being in time past Gentiles in the flesh . . . That at that time ye were without Christ, being . . . strangers from the covenants

> of promise, having no hope, and without God in the world. (Ephesians 2:11-12)

What will happen to the false gods, which have no life in them? Jeremiah tells of their future:

> The gods that have not made the heavens and the earth, even they shall perish from the earth, and from under these heavens. (Jeremiah 10:11)

Native Americans & the Missionaries

Native American author and lecturer for the Indigenous People's Movement, Richard Twiss, teaches that the Gospel was a "source of division and stumbling block for First Nations peoples and this is to be blamed on Western missionaries."[14]

In a sense, Twiss is partially correct in saying that the Gospel was a source of division. It was, and it still is! Quoting from the Old Testament, listen to what Paul says about Jesus:

> Behold, I lay in Sion a stumblingstone and a rock of offence: and whosoever believeth on him shall not be ashamed. (Romans 9:33)

And Jesus said:

> Suppose ye that I am come to give peace on earth? I tell you, Nay; but rather division. (Luke 12:51)

It is true that the Gospel does divide. It divides truth from error.

Western missionaries did lead First Nations people to God through the Gospel and still do today. But the World Christian Gathering of Indigenous Peoples (WCGIP) teach the traditions of men and belittle those faithful missionaries who gave of themselves to lovingly share the Gospel with the First Nations and Native American people. Sandy Simpson explains that while there were some "misguided missionaries" who tried to "change indigenous cultural values to Western ones," the IPM leaders "ignored the many missionaries who, in presenting the Gospel and sound doctrine, necessarily preached things that were in opposition to demonic cultures and practices like those of the Indians."[15] Simpson explains further:

> The missionaries were faced with heathen cultures, not unlike their own in the past, and attempted to apply biblical principles, in cooperation with those in First Nations, to come up with a way of living in accordance to the Word of God. . . .
>
> Mistakes were made, but if you talked to the first generation of converts . . . you would understand fully what First Nation's cultures were like at the time. Sexual perversion, women and child abuse, murder, human sacrifice, ruling elite who lorded it over everyone else, worship of demons, and other atrocities were commonplace. Those who heard the Gospel preached to them and recognized the freedom in Christ offered were saved and delivered from the evil in their cultures.[16]

The IPM leadership does not understand what these cultures were like before the missionaries came. Simpson also states:

> [The missionaries] were not sent to bring culture nor was that their purpose. They were primarily bringing God's values, the Bible, and applying its time-tested truths, together with First Nations peoples, so that they might be light and salt to the nations.[17]

Terry LeBlanc, a leader in the Indigenous People's Movement, tries to convince people that the "American Indians were not worshiping different gods or worshiping incorrectly before the missionaries brought to them Christ."[18] LeBlanc states:

> There's a myth that we have labored under for centuries in indigenous communities and the myth is that we are a godless heathen people.[19]

What the IPM is teaching in their vilifying of missionaries is a tactic also used by leaders in the emerging church movement, which convinces people that the former or biblical way of doing things is inherently bad. This is the platform they use to introduce radical new ideas to create a paradigm shift that is, unfortunately, unbiblical and leads people further and further from the Gospel message of salvation.

A book that I recently wrote the foreword to is titled *Stories From Indian Wigwams and Northern Campfires*. The book was written by a Canadian missionary who lived for many years among the Cree people in Manitoba in the late 1800s. When you hear Egerton Ryerson Young's account of his life with the Cree as a missionary, it is a much different account than what is being told in North American public school history books and by groups like the Indigenous People's Movement. In the foreword of Young's book, I wrote:

"[T]he Gospel was shared with Natives, including medicine men, which so often resulted in decisions being made for Jesus Christ. . . . [Mr. Young] shares very extraordinary events as he journeys to the remotest parts of Canada sharing the Gospel to the lost. He describes witnessing boldly to medicine men regarding their pagan beliefs with very encouraging and positive results achieved by no other than the Holy Spirit.

"Young tells [a] story of an old Chief who was taught the truth by a missionary regarding his belief in paganism. The missionary urged him to renounce this pagan, mystical spirituality and become a Christian. The old Chief was aware that he was a great sinner and needed a Savior. What an illustration this story is to show that God has placed in each of our hearts a conscience to know right from wrong.

"[T]he Gospel is indeed for everyone, and a loving God desires that none should perish without hearing about the Gospel (2 Peter 3:9). God does not accept the diverse spirituality of all cultures as being locked into truth. For Him to accept false and contradictory spirituality, while the Gospel calls all to repentance and belief in the Savior, would make God a liar—because there can only be one truth. And God cannot tell a lie because He is just and holy."[20]

Young's book left a deep impression on me in a particularly special way. After reading it, I realized that he had been a missionary to the Cree people of Manitoba, which is exactly where my ancestors came from. It is very possible that Young shared the Gospel with some of whom I am related to. In the back of my book, Appendix III gives one of the stories from Young's book. It's a moving account about a Cree chief named Maskepetoon. After I had read this story in Young's book, I remembered the name Maskepetoon from when I had done a family genealogy and had learned that Maskepetoon was my great, great grandfather Chief Kehiwin's best friend! At one point, I thought I was a descendant, but I was unable to know for sure. The reason I am including Maskepetoon's story in *Muddy Waters* is because it is an illustration of what the Scripture says in Romans:

> How beautiful are the feet of them that preach the gospel of peace, and bring glad tidings of good things! (Romans 10:15)

What is being taught in the new "emerging" way of doing missions (or the "new missiology") is that we cannot teach that salvation is the finished work of the Cross and that we must incorporate any unredeemable "articles of affection" to godly worship such as: fetishes, tobacco, peyote, sweet grass, drums, prayer feathers, frenzied dances, etc.

But to do so is idolatry in God's eyes and is blatant syncretism, from which we need to repent if we have engaged in these forbidden practices. We are redeemed and purified only by the blood of Jesus Christ, not through man-made efforts such as sweats, smudging ceremonies or via any ritual or ceremony. Jesus Christ paid the penalty for our sins on the Cross and declared, "It is finished!" Therefore, no other avenue is available, by which we can be purified or redeemed. Remember, there is only one mediator between God and man, Jesus Christ Himself (1 Timothy 2:5). But look what He promises those who remain true in standing in the faith:

> Let us be glad and rejoice, and give honour to him: for the marriage of the Lamb is come, and his wife [the saints] hath made herself ready. And to her was granted that she should be arrayed in fine linen, clean and white: for the fine linen is the righteousness of saints. And he saith unto me, Write, Blessed are they which are called unto the marriage supper of the Lamb. (Revelation 19: 7-9)

Titus Coan was a missionary in the 1830s to the Hawaiian Native people. Though he is little known today, some say he was the greatest missionary who ever lived. His is another example of the contrast between biblical missionaries to the Native people and the new missiology that is being presented by Leon Siu, Richard Twiss, John Dawon, Terry LeBlanc and the other IPM leaders. In this account by Coan, it's not difficult to see what happens when the true biblical Gospel is preached:

> At one place where I preached, there was an old and hardened Chief, who neither feared God nor regarded man. I preached to him fearlessly, personally, pointedly, calling him by name, and in the presence of his people. I charged home his guilt upon him, and in the name of the Lord urged him to immediate repentance. He was much moved, and promised repentance the first day, but I was not satisfied that his proud heart was broken.
>
> On the second day I renewed the charge. He stood the siege for awhile, but at length his feelings became insuppressible, and all on a sudden he broke forth in a cry that almost rent the heavens. The sword of the Spirit was in his veins. He submitted on the spot, and appears like a newborn

> babe. The effect of this scene on the congregation was overwhelming. The place was shaken. Multitudes cried out for mercy, and multitudes turned to the Lord. I could tell you of many similar facts. God has done great things for us. I feel like lying in the dust and adoring His grace.[21]

Oh that more missionaries today could have such zeal and confidence in the Gospel of Jesus Christ. It is that glorious thing that washes away all our sins and gives us garments of purity and cleanness to wear for eternity.

THE TOWER OF BABEL

This brings us back to Genesis 11:3-4 where the people decided to build a temple or ziggurat (ziggurats looked like pyramids with steps or ramps leading up the sides), which was built as a monument to their own greatness. In verse 4, the tower was a great human achievement to the people themselves and not to God. We often build monuments to ourselves such as those described above. It can be in the form of expensive clothing, fancy vehicles, huge homes, or jobs with titles that we use to give us identity and self-worth. Yet when we do this, we are usurping God from His rightful place in our lives. Are there "towers" like this in your life? It's a question we should all be asking ourselves. Since the attempt to build the tower of Babel, man has never ceased in his attempts to attain greatness and stature.

Cultural spirituality, with its many traditions, is not supported by Scripture; rather we are met with God's consistent warnings throughout the Bible, one of which is found in Colossians:

> Beware lest anyone cheat you through philosophy and empty deceit according to the traditions of men, according to the basic principles of the world, and not according to Christ. (Colossians 2:8)

And in the Gospel of Mark, we find:

> Making the Word of God of no effect through your traditions which you have handed down. And many such things you do. (Mark 7:13)

In an article titled "Listening Circle Brings Together Two Cultures," Mennonite writer Amy Dueckman states:

> About 90 people formed a circle—very important in Native culture—in the Emmanuel Mennonite Church gymnasium in Abbotsford the first evening to hear theologian Ray Aldred speak. Aldred . . . spoke on the topic, "How can traditional spirituality and understanding be fulfilled in the gospel, or transformed by it, in the same way that European cultures interpreted the gospel into their context?[22]

I pointed out earlier in chapter six that in Native culture the circle is very important and is representative of the idea that there really isn't any beginning or end to man or other created beings, and that a life just keeps going on and on (e.g. reincarnation). But God says nothing in His Holy Bible regarding circles as being an essential part of life. In fact, He says nothing about them at all, but

A ziggurat (tower)

we know that the Bible views human and animal life as having a definite physical beginning and end. From creation to the return of Jesus Christ our Lord, from the fall of man in Genesis to the new Heaven and the new earth, from the birth of a man until his death, God reveals a linear history filled with a purpose and an appointed time—to create new people for Himself.

The word 'culture' appears nowhere in the Bible from the beginning of Genesis to the end of Revelation. The Greek word *paradosis* translates into the English word "tradition." Pay careful attention to what God has to say about tradition in the following verses:

> Why do thy disciples transgress the tradition of the elders? for they wash not their hands when they eat bread. But he answered and said unto them, Why do ye also transgress the commandment of God by your tradition? . . . Thus have ye made the commandment of God of none effect by your tradition. (Matthew 15:2-3, 6)

Also see Matthew 15:2, 3, 6; Mark 7:3-13; and Colossians 2:8.

Man developed culture at Babel and passed down this same teaching to all generations to this apostate age in which we live. Grandpa used to share how the New Age (the New Spirituality) hijacked Native Spirituality. Yet, in all this, one thing remains certain—all unbiblical teaching originates from Babel.

The "redeeming the cultures" mindset:

> . . . permits the Word of God to be "contextualized" to a pagan culture through images, icons and symbols, thereby retaining the pagan elements of that culture. Using "redemptive analogies" (another heresy), these pagan beliefs and practices are claimed to be "redeemable" and are "christianized." Even the name of God is being changed to that of pagan deities![23]

The resurgence of Native Spirituality made a huge comeback because these traditions were kept alive in the underground world and originate from the age-old idolatry and witchcraft Deuteronomy 18:10-11 warns against. To blend error with truth results in damnable heresies resulting in swift destruction, which the Bible warns us strongly about:

> But there were false prophets also among the people, even as there shall be false teachers among you, who privily shall bring in damnable heresies, even denying the Lord that bought them, and bring upon themselves swift destruction. (2 Peter 2: 1)

Scripture gives no indication at all that we are to esteem the cultures or traditions of men. In Amy Dueckman's article about the circle event, she says:

> Opening the evening, members of the Sto:lo Coqualeetza Elders group of Chilliwack presented a special welcome with songs. Aldred then addressed the group, telling of his experiencing Christianity as a Native person who wondered if the Gospel was just for white people, or if it could speak to him, too. "When the Gospel is shared, it must be in the heart language of the people," he concluded. "Instead of telling [people] how to be Christian," he asked, "how about just telling them the story?"[24]

What story would that be? We do not have the authority to change the way we are to share the Gospel! We are commissioned to go and make disciples of all the nations, baptizing them in the name of the Father and of the Son and of the Holy Spirit. God is in the business of redeeming individual people that He might set apart a people for Himself. He did not say, "Go into the world and disciple the nations using stories!" The only story we are to share is the Good News of the Gospel of Jesus Christ and to preach Christ crucified!

Man's rebellion against God in Babel, following the flood, once again became a situation requiring God's judgment and intervention due to mankind's wickedness. Had God not confounded man's language, which in turn resulted in man being dispersed and disseminated into nations, man's wickedness only would have worsened with no end in sight. If you read from Genesis 1 to Genesis 11, you will read that God created man, birds, animals, fish, and creeping things. It does not say that He created cultures. God told the people to be fruitful and multiply. Man disobeyed, and instead, in his rebellion, man attempted to build a city to avoid being sent away. But God did just that anyway after they rebelled the second time by refusing to go forth and multiply (Genesis 10:30-32; Genesis 11:1-11). Man developed his own heathen traditions and passed down this teaching at Babel. In the Old Testament, plenty of evidence exists where God told the Israelites what they should do about other gods that were worshiped within the constructs of other belief systems (other cultures):

> And in all things that I have said unto you be circumspect: and make no mention of the name of other gods, neither let it be heard out of thy mouth. (Exodus 23:13)

> For all the gods of the nations are idols: but the LORD made the heavens. (Psalm 96:5)

> When thou art come into the land which the LORD thy God giveth thee, thou shalt not learn to do after the abominations of those nations. (Deuteronomy 18:9)

> That ye come not among these nations, these that remain among you; neither make mention of the name of their gods, nor cause to swear by them, neither serve them, nor bow yourselves unto them. (Joshua 23:7)

The Name of God

According to some Native Spiritual practitioners that I know personally, including people from other religions, we worship the same God regardless of what name we use to call God. In 2011, an emergent church group held A Symposium on Progressive Christianity. Progressive Christianity is another way of saying non-biblical Christianity. From an interview that was part of the symposium, the following excerpt is quite revealing as to the mindset of the "progressives":

> How should progressive Christians relate to other kinds of Christians? To those of other faiths? And what is their theological basis for so doing? We should always be willing to join hands for the common good and understanding of God. I personally believe that it doesn't matter the name you use to call God (how many names are attributed to God in our bible alone?)—even if your name for God is "Science," as long as you're on the same journey of grace, justice, and inclusion you are our brother/sister and we are honored to walk alongside of you. . . . If they're following God by practicing love, justice, and inclusion, then we're truly following the same God—even if we happen to be on different paths.[25]

Scripture mentions only two paths by which we will choose to walk in the Gospel of Matthew:

> Enter ye in at the strait gate: for wide is the gate, and broad is the way, that leadeth to destruction, and many there be which go in thereat. (Matthew 7:13)

The name of God that we use does matter according to the following Scripture:

> Neither is there salvation in any other: for there is none

> other name under heaven given among men, whereby we must be saved. (Acts 4: 12)

In Native Spirituality, there is the Great Spirit, but no such mention is found in the Bible; the Holy Spirit is mentioned, but He is part of the Trinity (Father, Son and Holy Spirit) and is NEVER called or referred to as the Great Spirit. In Native Spiritual teachings, their god, the Great Spirit, has neither a Father nor a Son. They do not preach redemption, salvation, sanctification, justification, repentance, etc. This confirms that the two are two different Spirits; one belongs to a Holy Trinity (Holy Spirit) and the other an unholy spirit (Great Spirit). The Great Spirit is severely lacking and devoid of holiness or of any true biblical doctrine but does have a doctrine of demons.

> Howbeit then, when ye knew not God, ye did service unto them which by nature are no gods.(Galatians 4:8)

If you take a look at names of God from Scripture in Appendix II, you will not find the Great Spirit listed there; neither will you find ancestors, grandfathers, etc. listed either in Scripture because as Christians, we do not worship the same God as many people would suggest to us.

In the Book of Acts, there is an account of Paul when he preached at Mars Hill to a heathen people. He told them:

> Ye men of Athens, I perceive that in all things ye are too superstitious. For as I passed by, and beheld your devotions, I found an altar with this inscription, TO THE UNKNOWN GOD. Whom therefore ye ignorantly worship, him declare I unto you. God that made the world and all things therein, seeing that he is Lord of heaven and earth, dwelleth not in temples made with hands; Neither is worshipped with men's hands, as though he needed any thing, seeing he giveth to all life, and breath, and all things. (Acts 17: 22-25)

Paul came to declare to these people who were worshiping an unknown god that God *did* have a name. He then told them about the Creator of the universe and about the one whom God "hath raised him from the dead [Jesus Christ]."

The greatest test by which we can gauge teaching of any sort is by obeying 1 John 4:1 to "try [test] the spirits." God's test for recognizing His Spirit is centered on the deity of Jesus, not tradition. We are admonished in 1 John 4:2-3 not to embrace man-made teaching; and 2 Corinthians 6:14-18 tells us to be separate from unbelievers.

A "false Jesus" is being lifted up in this apostate hour to usher in as many people into various false gospels propitiated by different spirits today such as: the New Apostolic Reformation (NAR) and the World Christian Gathering of Indigenous Peoples. Not to mention: the Indigenous People's Movement, Word of Faith, Emergent Church, New Age/New Spirituality, and contemplative prayer (Spiritual Formation). In some way, shape, or form, elements of Native Spirituality are taught in most of the above movements, and its direction is heading toward a unified global religion that the Bible warns will happen in the last days before Christ returns. This is why the apostle Paul urgently cautioned Christians that "another Jesus," a "different gospel," and a "different spirit" would be sermonized and acknowledged by the undiscerning in the last days. A false ecumenical "Jesus" will arise and will fool a world that is looking for a Messiah for all faiths and persuasions. Even in all of this, the one true Messiah and Savior remains high and lifted up above all false gods and false Christs:

> Wherefore God also hath highly exalted him, and given him a name which is above every name: That at the name of Jesus every knee should bow, of things in heaven, and things in earth, and things under the earth. (Philippians 2:9-10)

Ten

LIVING WATERS

> He that believeth on me, as the scripture hath said, out of his belly shall flow rivers of living water. (John 7:38)

> And I heard another voice from heaven, saying, Come out of her, my people, that ye be not partakers of her sins, and that ye receive not of her plagues. (Revelation 18:4)

> According as he hath chosen us in him before the foundation of the world, that we should be holy and without blame before him in love. (Ephesians 1:4)

Living water flows and brings life whereas muddy water is foul, dank, and stagnant, and it brings death. Jesus Christ came so that we can have lives washed anew with the living water of His Holy Spirit and the Word of God. The Bible teaches that sin influences every part of our being from birth because we are children of Adam. Before rebirth, we are spiritually dead. The Bible says that when we become born again, He translates us from the kingdom of darkness to the kingdom of Light. Everything is made new, old things are passed away, and we become new creatures. In His mercy, He saves us and opens our spiritual eyes:

> And you hath he quickened, who were dead in trespasses and sins; Wherein in time past ye walked according to the course of this world, according to the prince

> of the power of the air, the spirit that now worketh in the children of disobedience: Among whom also we all had our conversation in times past in the lusts of our flesh, fulfilling the desires of the flesh and of the mind; and were by nature the children of wrath, even as others. But God, who is rich in mercy, for his great love wherewith he loved us, Even when we were dead in sins, hath quickened us together with Christ, (by grace ye are saved;). (Ephesians 2:1-5)

Salvation means to be rescued from danger and taken to a safe place.

When the Bible talks about the forgiveness of sin, the turning point is called justification. This means that God forgives us—the guilty ones—and declares us innocent because of the great exchange of our sins for Christ's atonement that happened on the Cross.

This exchange, or justification, happens instantaneously; we don't grow into it. That's why it's connected to the term "born again." It's a change from one state—being "unborn"—to another state—being reborn. The Bible also teaches that as we die with Christ we are raised with Christ (see Romans 6:3–9).

Once we are born anew, we grow in Christ. We don't grow in being forgiven; we are already forgiven. We don't grow into being born again; we *are* born again. But we do grow more and more to be like Christ through the power of the Holy Spirit, through the washing of the Word of God, and through God's hand and direction in our lives' circumstances—both in blessings and in trials:

> And we know that all things work together for good to them that love God, to them who are the called according to his purpose. (Romans 8:28).

This process is called sanctification. It's also called walking with the Lord or walking in the Spirit. This continues throughout a believer's life, and it's not a "happy-go-lucky" superficial Christianity.

More often than we would like, it involves suffering, trials, temptations, and sacrifices. Nevertheless, we can experience all these with the risen Lord's victory and presence in our lives. And He has promised never to leave us or forsake us (Hebrews 13:5).

It's also very important to realize that this is *not* a state of sinlessness. One of the devil's most effective snares for believers is the temptation to pretend. While we are children of God, we are also at the same time imperfect, fallible human beings. The Bible teaches that every human being has a sinful nature, but that for those who believe, the Lord Jesus' death on the Cross has destroyed that "old man" under Adam—that old citizenship in the kingdom of darkness. Colossians says:

> Who hath delivered us from the power of darkness, and hath translated us into the kingdom of his dear Son. (Colossians 1:13)

However, even though our citizenship in Satan's kingdom has ended, sin doesn't disappear. After our re-birth, a sinful nature is still active—the literal term is "flesh." The good news, however, is that now the believer is indwelt by the Holy Spirit, and by walking in the Spirit, a believer needs no longer to be controlled by sin (Romans 8:5, Galatians 5:16).

A new Christian is like an immigrant who has entered a new land and is unfamiliar with its laws and customs. And standing nearby is the devil trying to convince that new babe in Christ that he or she never really left, twisting the Word of God and hurling flaming darts (see 1 Peter 5:8).

First Timothy warns us that there are "seducing spirits" and "doctrines of devils" (demons) that deceive and cause some to "depart from the faith" (1 Timothy 4:1).

But the beautiful difference is that now, not only is the mighty and glorious indwelling presence of the Holy Spirit at work within us, He has given us "all things that pertain unto life and godliness" (2 Peter 1:3) and is working to transform and to prepare us to come into the full inheritance kept in Heaven for us (Jeremiah 31:33; Ezekiel 36:26–27; 2 Corinthians 3:3; 1 Peter 1).

God is in the process of renewing the mind of a believer and making him aware of what is pleasing and displeasing to Him. A great deal of the New Testament talks about putting to death the evil deeds of the body by the Spirit (Galatians 5, Romans 6, 8, Colossians 3) as well as renouncing and fleeing from the works of darkness. Repentance is a process that really means turning around in the mind and going in the complete opposite direction. And only God's Word, through the power and illumination of the Holy Spirit, can transform our minds (see Romans 12:2). This process of sanctification can be difficult indeed, especially for those who have been deceived by Satan specifically in this area of the occult, which is so powerful and increasing in such dominance these days.

This is why it is so important to discern the types of "spirituality" we practice. And that is why the Bible continuously warns the people of God against involvement in worldly and demonic spiritual practices. Christians must separate themselves entirely from any spiritual practice that involves trying to create mystical experiences, something that is clearly not approved of in the Bible. Ephesians warns us:

> See then that ye walk circumspectly, not as fools, but as wise, Redeeming the time, because the days are evil. (Ephesians 5:15–16)

THE VULNERABILITY OF THE UNBELIEVER TO SATAN

But what if you're not a Christian? An unbeliever who hasn't received salvation by faith in Christ Jesus basically belongs to Satan, and is unable to have freedom from sin and evil and know true peace and joy. That is because he is still in the "old country" under the spiritual headship of a sinful nature (the flesh) inherited from Adam. He is a slave to sin and cannot escape by his own efforts. It took Christ's death on the Cross and His resurrection to accomplish this.

Satan knows this and will do everything he can to keep unbelievers away from Christ, often by tempting them with such gifts as occult power or by convincing them to end their own lives. A two-part article titled "Suicide, Murder, and Death in the Occult" reveals how commonplace this is:

> Suicide seems to be a recurring theme in the world of the occult, especially in the case of those who attempt to leave their former practices.

The article goes on to state that:

> Many times there is a deliberate attempt by the spirits to induce suicide in an unwary person. If people are trying to leave the occult, they are told they will never be able to and that the only escape is to take their own life. Or they may become enamored with blissful descriptions of the wonders of the "next-life" and be lovingly urged to "come join us."[1]

It is not futile, however, for an unbeliever to call on the Lord Jesus Christ for help, deliverance, and salvation. The Lord hears the cry of the weak, the humble, the repentant, and the brokenhearted. If you are not born again and are suffering Satan's lies and assaults, call upon God. Seek Him. Put your trust in Jesus Christ alone for your salvation.

Nothing is stronger than the Lord Jesus Christ. He can break all bondages and rescue every soul that turns to Him by faith from the prison of sin, death, and the devil. Call upon Him, for:

> Neither is there salvation in any other: for there is none other name under heaven given among men, whereby we must be saved. (Acts 4:12)

RECEIVING THE FREE GIFT OF SALVATION

Do you want a new life? Do you long to have your sins forgiven and removed from you "as far as the east is from the west" as is promised in Psalm 103:12? Are you willing to humble yourself and to give over the lordship of your life to the Lord Jesus Christ and to Him alone? Seek Him. Pray. Call upon the Lord, and seek His grace. Scripture tells us:

> Let us therefore come boldly unto the throne of grace, that we may obtain mercy, and find grace to help in time of need. (Hebrews 4:16)

> Then shall ye call upon me, and ye shall go and pray unto me, and I will hearken unto you. And ye shall seek me, and find me, when ye shall search for me with all your heart. (Jeremiah 29:12-13)

Do you lack faith? Ask Him for faith. Jesus said, "Ask, and it shall be given you; seek, and ye shall find; knock, and it shall be opened unto you" (Matthew 7:7). Read the Bible, which tells us that "faith cometh by hearing, and hearing by the word of God" (Romans 10:17).

Following is a prayer to help you. This is *not* a magic formula. Feel free to substitute your own words and to ponder the sections that apply to you. Wait upon Him in humility for strength, understanding, and direction.

It is important to understand that just praying a prayer or "making a decision" does not automatically make you a Christian. Salvation is a work of grace through faith, when we put our trust in Christ and Him alone for salvation by the power of the Holy Spirit. It is He and He alone who can give you a new heart. But if your prayer is sincere, He is faithful and will save you:

> For by grace are ye saved through faith; and that not of yourselves: it is the gift of God: Not of works, lest any man should boast. (Ephesians 2:8–9)

> Therefore being justified by faith, we have peace with God through our Lord Jesus Christ: By whom also we have access by faith into this grace wherein we stand, and rejoice in hope of the glory of God. (Romans 5:1–2)

A Prayer Asking the Risen Lord Jesus Christ to be Your Savior and Lord

Father in Heaven, I come to You recognizing my great need for a permanent deliverance from my old way of life. I know I am separated from You by my own sinfulness and am facing Your judgment and am under Your wrath, but I believe You can give me a new heart and life more abundantly because You love me and sent Your only Son, the Lord Jesus Christ, to pay the penalty for my sin by dying on the Cross in my place.

Your Word says that if I believe in Jesus Christ that I will not perish but have everlasting life (John 3:16), for You have broken the power of sin and death.

Please forgive me of all my sins and take me out of the kingdom of darkness and into Your kingdom. Show me specifically what I must repent of and renounce. Please forgive me for: __________________ (ask the Lord to show you how to pray).

I pray now, almighty risen Lord Jesus Christ, for You to take full control of my life as my Savior and Lord (1 Timothy 1:1). You say in Your Word that You are standing at the door knocking and will come in to the heart of anyone who will open that door (Revelation 3: 20). Open my heart and mind to Your truth and fellowship. Fill me with Your Holy Spirit and give me the power to live a holy life. Protect me from the devil's wiles, teach me to pray, as well as how to read, understand, and apply Your Word. Root me in Your Word, and lead me to and establish me in sound biblical Christian fellowship; and help me to persevere and grow in Your grace and truth.

In Jesus Christ's holy name, I pray. Amen.

A Prayer for a Christian to Renounce Involvement In Other Religions and the Occult

Perhaps you consider yourself a Christian, but now you realize that your involvement in Native American Spirituality or other forms of unbiblical spirituality and occult practices are wrong.

What should you do?

1. First of all, renounce and totally cease any involvement in these practices and also any involvement with other people who have been doing these things with you. Like an alcoholic trying to stay dry, you don't want to keep visiting bars unless you're really called to be an evangelist and have received grace, power, and wisdom to be in such a situation without taking part again. You should only decide this with the help of experienced, godly Christian counsel. See the sample Prayer of Renunciation below.

2. The next step is to meet with a godly, biblically sound church leader(s) or mature believer(s) and confess this sin, asking for help and the assurance of God's forgiveness. Unfortunately, many of you may not have a biblically sound church or pastor near you. In such a case, you will have to pray and trust God with it. And He is very capable of handling the situation if you really are sincere.

The reason for such a meeting is twofold: (a) These are sins against the Body of Christ, as well as the Head of the Body—Jesus Christ. In a sense, you've been involved in a different body—a body not only of unbelievers but of followers of other religions (that is, other ways to seek God besides through Jesus Christ, the only mediator). I Corinthians 10:21 says that we cannot drink the cup of the Lord and the cup of demons too. We cannot take part in both the Lord's table and the table of demons. (b) In James, it is written:

> Confess your faults one to another, and pray one for

> another, that ye may be healed. The effectual fervent prayer of a righteous man availeth much. (James 5:16)

Following is a sample prayer to help you focus, but please don't think that merely praying it will automatically or magically set you free. Your prayer should come from your heart by the direction of the Holy Spirit. You may only need to pray parts of this prayer.

Seek the Lord for His guidance.

PRAYER OF RENUNCIATION

Heavenly Father, I come to You in the name of Your Son, the Lord Jesus Christ, and by the power of His shed blood.

I confess that I have ignorantly engaged in learning and practicing North American Native Spirituality. I have engaged in false worship and used curses to seek revenge by hurting people, even those who were innocent, and to seek reverence amongst people.

I ask You to forgive me for all these sins and to cleanse me in the precious blood of the Lord Jesus Christ.

I confess that I took oaths that were contrary to the commandments of the Word of God. I renounce all such vows, bondages, oppression, spells, and curses that I received through learning North American Native Spirituality and fellowshipping with shamans and all other practitioners, and I ask You to forgive me for doing this.

I ask You to destroy every one of these oaths in the mighty and powerful name of the living and resurrected Lord Jesus Christ.

Heavenly Father, I confess that I established soul ties with practitioners and elders that were contrary to the Word of God.

I confess that I have idolized shamans (elders), a false Jesus (Manitou), a false spirit (Great Spirit), and fellow practitioners, and I ask You to forgive me of these abominable sins that You so rightly call idolatry. Lord Jesus Christ, cleanse me of all these sins with Your precious blood. Thank You for cleansing me with Your shed blood.

Abba Father, please bind all the demons of this idolatry in

the name of the living Lord Jesus Christ. I renounce all teachings received in Native Spirituality. I vow to destroy any protection, fungus, tobacco, medicine bag(s), Native artifact(s), dream catchers, pipe(s), and braids of sweet grass, sage, juniper, cedar branches, abalone shell, or any receptacle used for worship—including any book, picture, personal item, or spiritual name pertaining to Native Spirituality. Heavenly Father, I pray for Your power and protection to enable me to complete the renunciation and thank You for Your grace by which I stand.

In the name of the Lord Jesus Christ, I ask You to forgive me for the sin of pride—Native pride. Forgive me for endorsing false teaching to which I yielded instead of looking to the Lord Jesus Christ for all my needs and to the Word of God for the truth. I confess as sin and renounce all fascination with, belief in, and practice of Native Spirituality and mind control techniques, ESP, chanting, power objects, necromancy, astral projection, trances, reincarnation, occult dreams and any other area of the occult. (Ask God to show you anything you may have missed.) I claim back from Satan all these areas to which I have opened doors and ask You, Father, to please bind and cast out in Jesus' name every demon connected with them. I renounce all passivity developed in the practice of Native Spirituality, including opening my mind without discerning good and evil. I pray to You to teach me the right use of my mind, will, and imagination. Heavenly Father, I confess as sin and renounce all involvement in sweat lodge ceremonies, pipe ceremonies, sacred and healing circles, sun dance ceremonies, writings, and oral teachings that are contrary to God's Word, in Jesus Christ's name. (Confess any other involvement that you may have had that is not listed here.)

Father, please remove, in the name of Jesus Christ, all the demons of these teachings in me, my spouse, and my family, and command them to leave forever and never bother us again.

Father, I renounce, in Jesus Christ's name, all teachings and traditional beliefs, all rituals that I have participated in—the naming ceremony, the sun dance ceremony, and so forth. (Ask

God to show you everything you need to renounce in this area.) Cleanse me, Lord Jesus Christ, of all these sins in your precious blood. Father, please bind and remove all spirits of death, including suicide, in the name of Jesus Christ and command them to leave me and my family now in the name of the living and risen Lord Jesus Christ.

Father, please bind and remove all spirits connected with Native Spirituality and command them to depart now forever and never to return, in Jesus Christ's all-powerful name. Father, I confess as sin and renounce all involvement with any forms of thinking or activities that have to do with animism-based worship and female superiority. I pray to be brought into line with Your Word in all areas that require Your truth.

In the name of the Lord Jesus Christ I declare, by faith, that I have been set free and washed in the precious blood of the Lamb. Abba Father, I ask that You would refresh the Holy Spirit's indwelling in me, and use me as an instrument of righteousness that You can complete Your good works in me and in others.

Father in Heaven, open my eyes to see how great Your ways are compared to mine and to desire Your ways only. Help me to walk only in Your paths, Lord, and to put on the full armor of God. Fill me with Your Holy Spirit and give me power, wisdom, and endurance to faithfully follow You.

You say in 1 John 1:9 that if I confess my sin, You will be faithful and just to forgive me and purify me from all unrighteousness. I thank You for that. I believe in the name of the all-powerful, all-knowing Lord Jesus Christ Who is able to accomplish these things.

The battle of transformation into holiness is not won in a day. But God's promise is certain. He will form Christ in you (Galatians 4:19) as you surrender your life to Him. And He promises to change us:

> But we all, with open face beholding as in a glass the glory of the Lord, are changed into the same image

> from glory to glory, even as by the Spirit of the Lord. (2 Corinthians 3:18)

Persevere! The important thing is that you are praying to the Living God.

May God bless you!

PUT ON THE FULL ARMOR OF GOD

Finally, the apostle Paul tells Christians to be strong in the Lord and in His mighty power and to put on the full armor of God[2] so we can stand against the "wiles of the devil" (Ephesians 6:11).

What is this armor, and how do we put it on and stand?

NOTE: Only a born-again Christian can truly walk in the armor God provides in Ephesians 6:10–18. If you do not know Jesus Christ as your personal Savior and have not accepted Him as Lord and Savior of your life (2 Peter 1:11, 2 Peter 2:20), it will only be a meaningless ritual. If you are a Christian who desires to return to the Lord, contemplating the meaning of each piece of the armor can be an aid to drawing nearer to the Lord and walking in the Holy Spirit. To receive the full armor of God, I present this prayer as a general guideline. Use only what applies.

Father in Heaven, thank You that the "weapons of our warfare are not carnal, but mighty through God to the pulling down of strong holds" (2 Corinthians 10:4). Enable me, Father, through the power of Your Holy Spirit and in the name of our Lord Jesus Christ, to find my strength in You and in Your mighty power and to put on Your complete armor so that I can stand in the warfare I encounter and be faithful and fully equipped to endure to the end.

> Finally, my brethren, be strong in the Lord and in the power of His might. Put on the whole armor of God, that ye may be able to stand against the wiles of the devil. (Ephesians 6:10-11)

I confess that as a child of God, through the completed work of the death and resurrection of Jesus Christ, I have died, been born again, and am now a solid citizen of the kingdom of Heaven. As such, I have victory over sin's domination and all of Satan's realm. Thank You Lord that my strength comes from what the Lord Jesus Christ accomplished through His death, resurrection, and glorification. I ask forgiveness for and renounce every other means of obtaining strength: (ask God to reveal to you what they are).

In the name of the Lord Jesus Christ and through the power of His Cross in my life, I renounce and willingly bring to the Cross all forms of my sinful nature (ask God to show you what they are and pray them here: fear, lust, impurity, selfish ambition, and so on).

NOTE: Our battle against the flesh is an ongoing daily struggle and will continue until we've gone home to be with the Lord in Heaven. Do not expect to become perfect on earth! But, although we cannot have perfection now, we can know His victory through our walk in the Holy Spirit. And we must remember the nature of this battle:

> For we wrestle not against flesh and blood, but against principalities, against powers, against the rulers of the darkness of this world, against spiritual wickedness in high places. (Ephesians 6:12)

Lord, please open my eyes to the true nature of the warfare I am in and show me any ways in which I am battling in my own power or in the power of Satan. Give me discernment to recognize the spiritual forces at work behind events and relationships and help me not merely to react but to wait upon You for guidance. Please protect me by the precious blood of my Lord Jesus Christ from all wrong involvements, spiritual entanglements, and teachings.

> Wherefore take unto you the whole armour of God, that ye may be able to withstand in the evil day, and having done all, to stand. Stand therefore, having your loins

> girt about with truth, and having on the breastplate of righteousness. (Ephesians 6:13–14)

Lord, I acknowledge that sin's power and the devil have been defeated through the Lord Jesus' death and resurrection and that as a child of God I can walk in that truth and victory. I put on the girdle of truth by faith and ask You to help me walk in it daily.

Show me any weaknesses in my faith and understanding of Your Holy Word and illuminate the Word for me. Show me any areas of my life where I am being tossed about by winds of doctrine (Ephesians 4:14) or where I am following unbiblical philosophies. Show me if I am relying more on power than truth in facing the battles in my life.

Help me stand on the rock of Your Word. I renounce every way in which I am leaning on my own understanding or perception of righteousness instead of what the Lord Jesus Christ has provided for me through *His* righteousness. For in the verses below we are told:

> But we are all as an unclean thing, and all our righteousnesses are as filthy rags. (Isaiah 64:6)

> There is none righteous, no, not one. (Romans 3:10)

I confess that neither exalted nor subjective experiences, works, feelings, nor emotions can save me, but only by the righteousness that comes through the Lord Jesus Christ can I be saved. Show me, Lord, any snares I have fallen into, where my emotions are unbalanced, if my conscience is unresponsive or confused, and if I am exercising my will incorrectly. Show me if I am being too passive or complacent, spiritually. Teach me the right use of my mind and will.

Pray the following if you think you are not saved when you sin:

Help me to grasp the crucial difference between being saved and being made holy, between Christ's righteousness that I received at my salvation and the daily process of sanctification that will go on until I join You in Heaven. In the mighty name of the risen Lord Jesus Christ, I resist the devil's trick to fool me into thinking I'm not saved when I am.

Lord, please show me where I have not been standing firm or in Your strength. Show me if and where I have been compromising Your Word, and if one of my feet is in You Lord and the other is in the world (or if I have allowed a false spirituality such as Eastern religion to enter in). I ask forgiveness for and renounce _______________ (whatever the Lord shows you). Now I put on the sandals of the Gospel of peace so that I am mobile, sturdy, and stable. "And your feet shod with the preparation of the gospel of peace" (Ephesians 6:15).

Guide my feet along Your paths, Lord, and help me to take "the shield of faith, wherewith [I] shall be able to quench all the fiery darts of the wicked" (Ephesians 6:16).

Lord, please show me the specific fiery darts the enemy is hurling at me at this time, as well as any to which I have succumbed in the past. I hold up the shield of faith and proclaim Your total sovereignty, Your faithfulness, and Your provision for me. I ask for Your specific help for: (whatever the Lord shows you). Show me the Scriptures that are best suited to help me resist these attacks and help me to persevere until I achieve victory. May I remember to "take the helmet of salvation, and the sword of the Spirit, which is the word of God" (Ephesians 6:17).

Lord, I place upon my head by faith Your helmet of salvation, the hope of glory. Refresh and renew my spiritual vision. Help me to look up and keep ever before me the glorious inheritance You have prepared for me. Protect my mind, my understanding, and my intellect from all that is corrupt and that would deaden my awareness of my ultimate goal in Christ Jesus. Help me to continue even when I grow very weary.

Lord, I take hold of Your Word by faith as my sharp sword. Please place in my heart a burning hunger for it, a thirst that will not be quenched, except by more and more truth. Show me the areas where I am weak and bring me into contact with good, faithful Bible teaching. Help me to be alert to the devil's sudden attacks and empower me to wield Your sword of truth diligently, faithfully, powerfully, and quickly in every situation. Help me to be effectual and fervent (James 5:16) in prayer and faith for Your name's sake.

In the mighty name of the Lord Jesus Christ, I reclaim all the areas Satan has taken in my life: _______________ and ask You to cleanse me from all ground I've given to him, which have been strongholds in my life.

> Praying always with all prayer and supplication in the Spirit, and watching thereunto with all perseverance and supplication for all saints." (Ephesians 6:18)

I confess and ask forgiveness for my weakness in prayer as follows: _______________. Fill me with Your Holy Spirit and give me a burning spirit of prayerful communion with You, including watchfulness and wakefulness both for myself and for others. Enable me to pray "without ceasing" (1 Thessalonians 5:17) in accordance with Your will, to persevere in prayer and never give up.

> And for me, that utterance may be given unto me, that I may open my mouth boldly, to make known the mystery of the gospel, For which I am an ambassador in bonds: that therein I may speak boldly, as I ought to speak. (Ephesians 6:19–20)

Lord, I praise You for the fellowship of the saints, for that great body of which I am a part. If I have been out of fellowship with believers, I ask your help in being faithful and persevering.[3] Place and firmly establish me in that part of the Body of Christ that is Your good and perfect will for me. Help me to pray always for my brothers and sisters in the Lord.

Wisdom, boldness, and courage—Lord, I ask for them all

so that I can fearlessly proclaim Your truth at every opportunity.

Thank You, Lord, for the reality of this armor and for giving me the strength and grace to walk in it. I know I cannot walk with You on my own strength. Give me great endurance to persevere to the end.

All glory belongs to You, mighty God: Father, Son, and Holy Spirit, now and forevermore. Amen.

Stand fast therefore in the liberty wherewith Christ hath made us free, and be not entangled again with the yoke of bondage. (Galatians 5:1)

That he might present it to himself a glorious church, not having spot, or wrinkle, or any such thing; but that it should be holy and without blemish. (Ephesians 5:27)

Afterword

If the statistics are true, only about five percent of Native Americans call themselves Christian. I hope that number is wrong. Like many Jews, I know there is good reason why Natives feel bitterness toward the white Christian, calling Christianity the white man's religion. There have been great injustices done to Native Americans as there have been to the Jews in the name of Christianity. Even today, prejudice is still all too common. But those who persecuted and prejudged Native Americans, Blacks, or Jews and called themselves Christian were committing a horrible misrepresentation of Jesus Christ and true Christianity. Biblical Christianity teaches us to love our neighbor as ourselves and that God is no respecter of persons. He loves and cares for people of *all* ethnic backgrounds.

I realize reading *Muddy Waters* may anger some Native Americans because I have stated strongly my belief that Native Spirituality is spiritually harmful and will not lead to living waters and solid ground but will only lead to muddy waters and cause its adherents to be on dangerous ground. Only one thing will help the Native American, just like only one thing will help the Jew, the Black, the Hispanic, or the White, and that is believing on and loving the Lord Jesus Christ with all of your heart, mind, and soul, along with surrendering your will and your entire life to him.

I will leave you with this excerpt from Egerton Ryerson Young (missionary to the Cree People of Manitoba in the late 1800s):

By Egerton Ryerson Young

Missionary work among the Indians, like that in all lands, has its hours of sadness and discouragement as well as of hope and rejoicing. We look back with thankfulness that it was not only our privilege to go forth weeping, bearing the precious seed, but that in addition the Master of the harvest gave us the joy of the reapers. It was our great happiness to see "many a sheaf both ripe and golden" gathered in. The work was one of peculiar hardships to both Mrs. Young and myself, but the conversion of scores of souls every year amply repaid us for the sufferings and anxieties of that life so isolated and lonely as it must necessarily be in mission fields so far from civilization. Many encouraging incidents were constantly occurring to cheer the hearts of the lonely toilers and to stimulate them to labor on in the blessed work. It is a joy to record some of these trophies won not only through our own feeble instrumentality, but also through the loving, consecrated efforts of our loved brother missionaries. One of these dear brethren, writing, says:

> A young Indian who was very sick had his friends bring him twenty-five miles to the home of the missionary. He wept when he came into his presence, and said he wanted to learn about Jesus before he died. He said, 'I am very wicked, and I want to get a new heart.' When urged to pray he replied, 'I can't pray; I don't know how.' The faithful missionary, with a conscious sense of the nearness and infinite compassion of the Divine One, earnestly pointed him to the Lamb of God. Next day, when the missionary called upon him, the poor sick man, holding out his hand, exclaimed with rapture, 'Jesus has heard my prayer and made my heart good. Now pray for wife also.' He began from that time to recover from his sickness, and a few days later his wife also accepted Christ as her Saviour, and now both are rejoicing in Jesus.

A beautiful story is told by one of our earlier Indian missionaries of a proud and powerful chief who, under the preaching of the Gospel, became deeply convicted of sin. Trembling under a sense of his guilt, he came to the missionary and offered him his much-prized belt of wampum to have his load of guilt removed.

When told that the Lord Jesus did not want this offering he went away very sad and depressed in spirit. Soon after he returned and offered his gun and favorite dog. "These are not what Christ wants," said the missionary. Again he went away sorrowful, but after a time he returned and offered his wigwam and family. The faithful missionary, who saw the struggle that was going on in his heart, refused for his Master even these, saying that "the Saviour could not accept even these as a sacrifice for sin." The poor convicted, half-despairing Indian then threw himself down upon the ground, and, lifting up his tearful eyes, exclaimed, "Here, Lord, I can do no more. Please take poor Indian too." The answer of peace and pardon was not long in coming.

Many more delightful instances could be given of the Gospel's power to save . . . How true it is that it is not always that the greatest results for God are obtained when the surroundings are most favorable! The crowded, enthusiastic audience does not always yield the greatest number of converts. How often has it been seen by the faithful minister or devoted Sunday-school teacher that their work seemed specially owned of God when under difficulties and discouragements they sacrificed self and personal comfort to be in their place and do their duty!

Many can look back to some cold, wet Sunday or other apparently very unfavorable time, from the human stand-point, when, because they were in their place, precious immortal souls were then influenced by the truth and heartily, believingly accepted Christ as their personal, conscious Saviour. Little did I dream, as I stood up before the little company on that Dakota prairie and preached that short, simple sermon, that it was to be one of the successful sermons of my life (from chapter IX, *Stories From Indian Wigwams and Northern Campfires*).

TERMINOLOGY

First Nations people—Many people today prefer to be called "First Nations" or "First Nations people" instead of "Indians." Generally, the term First Nations is used to describe both Status and Non-Status Indians. The term is rarely used as a synonym for "Aboriginal peoples" because it usually doesn't include Inuit or Métis people.

Indian—The term "Indian" collectively describes all the Indigenous people in Canada who are not Inuit or Métis. Indian peoples are one of three peoples recognized as Aboriginal in the Constitution Act, 1982. It specifies that Aboriginal people in Canada consist of the Indian, Inuit, and Métis peoples.

There are three categories of Indians in Canada: Status Indians, Non-Status Indians and Treaty Indians.

Status Indians—Status Indians are people who are entitled to have their names included on the Indian Register, an official list maintained by the federal government. Certain criteria determine who can be registered as a Status Indian. Only Status Indians are recognized as Indians under the Indian Act, which defines an Indian as "a person who, pursuant to this Act, is registered as an Indian or is entitled to be registered as an Indian." Status Indians are entitled to certain rights and benefits under the law.

Non-Status Indians—Non-Status Indians are people who consider themselves Indians or members of a First Nation but whom the Government of Canada does not recognize as Indians under the Indian Act, either because they are unable to prove their status or have lost their status rights. Many Indian people in Canada, especially women, lost their Indian status through discriminatory practices in the past. Non-Status Indians are not entitled to the same rights and benefits available to Status Indians.

Treaty Indian—A Status Indian who belongs to a First Nation that signed a treaty.

Inuit—An Aboriginal people in Northern Canada, who live in Nunavut, Northwest Territories, Northern Quebec and Northern Labrador. The word means "people" in the Inuit language — Inuktitut. The singular of Inuit is Inuk.

Métis—People of mixed First Nation and European ancestry who identify themselves as Métis, as distinct from First Nations people, Inuit or non-Aboriginal people. The Métis have a unique culture that draws on their diverse ancestral origins, such as Scottish, French, Ojibwa, and Cree.

APPENDIX I
UNEQUAL CONTENDERS IN THE SPIRITUAL WAR

God and Satan are not two equal powers in a dualistic battle between good and evil. God's power is infinite whereas Satan can only do what the Lord gives him permission to do, as evidenced in the Book of Job. Therefore, Satan's power is limited whereas God's power is without limit. Our Lord reigns as the supreme Creator and King of the universe, and His purposes are being accomplished in the world whether or not His creatures accept Him as Lord. The information on the following pages illustrates the relationship between God and His creation.*

ETERNAL
GOD He is before all things. (Colossians 1:17)
MAN For he that soweth to his flesh shall of the flesh reap corruption; but he that soweth to the Spirit shall of the Spirit reap life everlasting." (Galatians 6:8)
SATAN And the devil that deceived them was cast into the lake of fire and brimstone, where the beast and the false prophet are, and shall be tormented day and night for ever and ever. (Revelation 20-9-11)

*Most of the material from Appendix I has been taken from Kjos Ministries website, used with permission. You may view this and other valuable information at: http://www.crossroad.to/charts/spiritual_war.htm

KING

GOD

I am Alpha and Omega, the beginning and the end, the first and the last. (Revelation 22:13)

MAN

Then we which are alive and remain shall be caught up together with them in the clouds, to meet the Lord in the air: and so shall we ever be with the Lord. (1 Thessalonians 4:17)

SATAN

. . . an angel come down from heaven . . . laid hold on the dragon, that old serpent, which is the Devil, and Satan, and bound him . . . And the devil that deceived them was cast into the lake of fire and brimstone. (Revelation 20:1-2, 10)

SHEPHERD

GOD

I am the good shepherd: the good shepherd giveth his life for the sheep. (John 10:11)

MAN

God is faithful, who will not suffer you to be tempted above that ye are able; but will with the temptation also make a way to escape, that ye may be able to bear it. (1 Corinthians 10:13)

SATAN

Be sober, be vigilant; because your adversary the devil, as a roaring lion, walketh about, seeking whom he may devour. (1 Peter 5:8)

The thief cometh not, but for to steal, and to kill, and to destroy: I am come that they might have life, and that they might have it more abundantly. (John 10:10)

LORD

GOD

The LORD is my rock, and my fortress, and my deliverer; my God, my strength, in whom I will trust; my buckler, and the horn of my salvation, and my high tower. (Psalm 18:2)

Which in his times he shall shew, who is the blessed and only Potentate, the King of kings, and Lord of lords. (1 Timothy 6:15)

MAN

Rejected His Lordship: And when the woman saw that the tree was good for food, and that it was pleasant to the eyes, and a tree to be desired to make one wise, she took . . . and did eat, and gave . . . to her husband . . . and he did eat. (Genesis 3:6)

SATAN

Deceives people through lies, threats, deception, twisted truths and counterfeit promises . . . [F]or Satan himself is transformed into an angel of light. (2 Corinthians 11:14)

. . . the snare of the devil, who are taken captive by him at his will. (2 Timothy 2:26)

JUDGE

GOD

Before the LORD: for he cometh, for he cometh to judge the earth: he shall judge the world with righteousness, and the people with his truth. (Psalm 96:13)

MAN

Faced with spiritual death and bondage as a consequence for sin. (See Genesis 2:17 and Romans 4:12.)

SATAN

Charged with rebellion. How art thou fallen from heaven, O Lucifer, son of the morning! how art thou cut down to the ground, which didst weaken the nations! . . . Yet thou shalt be brought down to hell, to the sides of the pit. (Isaiah 14:12, 15)

CREATOR

GOD

For by him were all things created, that are in heaven, and that are in earth, visible and invisible . . . all things were created by him, and for him. (Colossians 1:16)

MAN

God created man in his own image. (Genesis 1:27, Psalm 2)

SATAN

Created, as an angel, to serve and minister but chose to rebel and rule: For thou hast said in thine heart, I will ascend into heaven, I will exalt my throne above the stars of God: I will sit also upon the mount of the congregation, in the sides of the north: I will ascend above the heights of the clouds; I will be like the most High. (Isaiah 14:13-14)

SAVIOR

GOD

[W]e . . . know that this is indeed the Christ, the Saviour of the world. (John 4:42)

But he was wounded for our transgressions, he was bruised for our iniquities: the chastisement of our peace was upon him; and with his stripes we are healed. (Isaiah 53:5)

MAN

For the wages of sin is death; but the gift of God is eternal life through Jesus Christ our Lord. (Romans 6:23)

He came unto his own, and his own received him not. But as many as received him, to them gave he power to become the sons of God. (John 1:11-12)

That whosoever believeth in him should not perish, but have eternal life. (John 3:15)

SATAN

Has limited access to faithful believers: Be sober, be vigilant; because your adversary the devil, as a roaring lion, walketh about, seeking whom he may devour: Whom resist stedfast in the faith, knowing that the same afflictions are accomplished in your brethren that are in the world. (1 Peter 5:8-9)

In God's economy, He takes what was meant for even the worst evil and works it all to His good: ". . . the devil having now put into the heart of Judas Iscariot, Simon's son, to betray him" (John 13:2).

VICTOR

GOD

In the world ye shall have tribulation: but be of good cheer; I have overcome the world. (John 16:33)

MAN

For I am persuaded, that neither death, nor life, nor angels, nor principalities, nor powers, nor things present, nor things to come, Nor height, nor depth, nor any other creature, shall be able to separate us from the love of God, which is in Christ Jesus our Lord. (Romans 8:38-39)

SATAN

. . . ought not this woman, being a daughter of Abraham, whom Satan hath bound . . . lo, these eighteen years, be loosed . . .? (Luke 13:16)

. . . healing all that were oppressed of the devil . . . (Acts 10:38)

Submit yourselves therefore to God. Resist the devil, and he will flee from you. (James 4:7)

PROVIDER

GOD

But my God shall supply all your need according to his riches in glory by Christ Jesus. (Philippians 4:19)

Wherefore, if God so clothe the grass of the field, which to day is, and to morrow is cast into the oven, shall he not much more clothe you, O ye of little faith? Therefore take no thought, saying, What shall we eat? or, What shall we drink? or, Wherewithal shall we be clothed? (For after all these things do the Gentiles seek:) for your heavenly Father knoweth that ye have need of all these things. (Matthew 6:30-32)

MAN

And God said, Behold, I have given you every herb bearing seed. (Genesis 1:29)

And I have led you forty years in the wilderness: your clothes are not waxen old upon you, and thy shoe is not waxen old upon thy foot. (Deuteronomy 29:5)

SATAN

Assigned limited power—yet ultimately accountable to God. And the LORD said unto Satan, Behold, all that he hath is in thy power; only upon himself put not forth thine hand. So Satan went forth from the presence of the LORD. (Job 1:12)

Therefore, Satan's power is but a droplet in the ocean of God's power!

APPENDIX II
NAMES FOR GOD

OLD TESTAMENT NAMES FOR GOD
(not a comprehensive list)

ADONAI—Lord and Master (Genesis 15:2)

EL-ECHAD—The One God (Malachi 2:10)

ELOHIM—God, Judge, Creator (Genesis 1:1, Psalm 29:1)

EL-OLAM—The Everlasting God, The God of Eternity, The God of the Universe, The God of Ancient Days (Jeremiah 10:10, Isaiah 40:28-31)

EL-ELYON—The Most High God (Isaiah 14:13-14)

EL-HAKKADOSH—The Holy God (Isaiah 5:16)

EL-ROI—The God Who Sees (Genesis 16:13)

EL-SHADDAI—Lord God Almighty (Genesis 48:3)

JEHOVAH-RAAH—The Lord, my Shepherd (Psalm 23:1)

JEHOVAH-SHAMMAH—The Lord is There (present) (Ezekiel 48:35)

JEHOVAH-RAPHA—The Lord that Heals (Exodus 15:26)

JEHOVAH-TSIDKENU—The Lord, our Righteousness (Jeremiah 23:6)

JEHOVAH-JIREH—The Lord will Provide (Genesis 22:13-14)

JEHOVAH-NISSI—The Lord, my Banner (Exodus 17:15)

JEHOVAH-SHALOM—The Lord is Peace (Judges 6:24)

JEHOVAH-SABBAOTH—The Lord of Hosts (Isaiah 6:1-3)

JEHOVAH-GMOLAH—The God Who Recompenses (Jeremiah 51:6)

MEKODDISHKEM—The Lord Who Sanctifies you (Exodus 31:13)

YAHWEH (or YHWH)—Lord, Jehovah, I Am Who I AM (Genesis 2:4)

MORE NAMES FOR GOD

ABBA FATHER—Romans 8:15
ADVOCATE—1 John 2:1
ALMIGHTY—Genesis 17:1
ALPHA & OMEGA—Revelation 22:13
AMEN—Revelation 3:14
ANCIENT OF DAYS—Daniel 7:9
ANOINTED ONE—Psalm 2:2
APOSTLE & HIGH PRIEST—Hebrews 3:1
AUTHOR & FINISH OF OUR FAITH—Hebrews 12:2

BEGINNING AND THE END—Revelation 21:6
BLESSED—1 Timothy 6:15
BRANCH OF RIGHTEOUSNESS—Jeremiah 33:15
BREAD OF GOD—John 6:33
BREAD OF LIFE—John 6:35
BRIDEGROOM—Matthew 5:25
BRIGHT & MORNING STAR—Revelation 22:16
BRIGHTNESS OF HIS GLORY—Hebrews 1:3

CHIEF SHEPHERD—1 Peter 5:4
CHRIST—Matthew 22:42
CHRIST OF GOD—Luke 9:20
CHRIST THE LORD—Luke 2:11
CHRIST, SON OF THE LIVING GOD—Matthew 16:16
COMFORTER—John 14:26
CONSUMING FIRE—Hebrews 12:29
CORNERSTONE—Isaiah 28:16
COUNSELOR—Isaiah 9:6
CREATOR—1 Peter 4:19

DELIVERER—Romans 11:26
DOOR OF THE SHEEP—John 10:7

ETERNAL GOD—Deuteronomy 33:27
EVERLASTING FATHER—Isaiah 9:6

FAITHFUL & TRUE—Revelation 19:11
FAITHFUL WITNESS—Revelation 1:5
FATHER—Matthew 6:9
FIRSTBORN—Romans 8:29
FIRSTFRUITS—1 Corinthians 15:20-23
FOUNDATION—1 Corinthians 3:11

GOOD SHEPHERD—John 10:11
GREAT HIGH PRIEST—Hebrews 4:14
GUIDE—Psalm 48:14

HEAD OF THE BODY—Colossians 1:18
HEAD OF THE CHURCH—Ephesians 5:23
HEIR OF ALL THINGS—Hebrews 1:2
HIGH PRIEST—Hebrews 3:1
HIGH PRIEST FOREVER—Hebrews 6:20
HOLY ONE—Acts 2:27
HOLY ONE OF ISRAEL—Isaiah 49:7
HOLY GHOST—Matthew 1:18
HOLY SPIRIT—Ephesians 4:30
HORN OF SALVATION—Luke 1:69

I AM—Exodus 3:14, John 8:58
IMAGE OF HIS PERSON—Hebrews 1:3
IMMANUEL—Isaiah 7:14

JESUS—Matthew 1:21
JESUS CHRIST OUR LORD—Romans 6:23
JUDGE—Acts 10:42

KING—Zechariah 9:9
KING ETERNAL—1 Timothy 1:17

KING OF KINGS—1 Timothy 6:15
KING OF SAINTS—Revelation 15:3

LAMB OF GOD—John 1:29
LAST ADAM—1 Corinthians 15:45
LAWGIVER—Isaiah 33:22
LIFE—John 14:6
LIGHT OF THE WORLD—John 8:12
LILY OF THE VALLEYS—Song of Solomon 2:1
LION OF THE TRIBE OF JUDAH—Revelation 5:5
LIVING STONE—1 Peter 2:4
LIVING WATER—John 4:10
LORD—John 13:13
LORD GOD ALMIGHTY—Revelation 15:3
LORD JESUS CHRIST—1 Corinthians 15:57
LORD OF ALL—Acts 10:36
LORD OF GLORY —1 Corinthians 2:8
LORD OF HOSTS—Haggai 1:5
LORD OF LORDS—1 Timothy 6:15

MAN OF SORROWS—Isaiah 53:3
MASTER—Luke 5:5
MEDIATOR—1 Timothy 2:5
MESSENGER OF THE COVENANT—Malachi 3:1
MESSIAS—John 4:25

NAZARENE—Matthew 2:23

OFFSPRING OF DAVID—Revelation 22:16
OMEGA—Revelation 22:13
ONLY BEGOTTEN SON—John 1:18
OUR PASSOVER—1 Corinthians 5:7
OUR PEACE—Ephesians 2:14

PRINCE OF LIFE—Acts 3:15 POTTER—Isaiah 64:8

POWER OF GOD—1 Corinthians 1:24
PRINCE OF PEACE—Isaiah 9:6
PRINCE OF THE KINGS OF THE EARTH—Revelation 1:5
PROPHET—Acts 3:22

RABBONI (TEACHER/MASTER)—John 20:16
REDEEMER—Job 19:25
REFINER'S FIRE—Malachi 3:2
RESURRECTION—John 11:25
RIGHTEOUS—1 John 2:1
ROCK—1 Corinthians 10:4
ROOT OF DAVID—Revelation 22:16
ROSE OF SHARON—Song of Solomon 2:1
RULER IN ISRAEL—Micah 5:2

SAVIOUR—Luke 2:11
SCEPTER OUT OF ISRAEL—Numbers 24:17
SHEPHERD OF OUR SOULS—1 Peter 2:25
SON OF DAVID (and ABRAHAM)—Matthew 1:1
SON OF GOD—Matthew 27:54
SON OF MAN—Matthew 8:20
SON OF THE HIGHEST—Luke 1:32
SPIRIT OF GOD—Genesis 1:2
STONE—1 Peter 2:8
SUN OF RIGHTEOUSNESS—Malachi 4:2

THE WORD OF GOD—Revelation 19:13
THE WORD—John 1:1
TRUE LIGHT—John 1:9
TRUE WITNESS—Revelation 3:14
TRUTH—John 14:6

WAY—John 14:6
WISDOM OF GOD—1 Corinthians 1:24
WONDERFUL—Isaiah 9:6

APPENDIX III
THE STORY OF MASKEPETOON

By Egerton Ryerson Young

The following incident occurred years ago on the great plains of the Canadian Northwest, long before the waves of Anglo-Saxon civilization began to surge over those glorious fertile prairies which for so many generations were hid from the gaze of the outside busy world. Among the Indian tribes that roamed over those vast regions the Crees in those days were perhaps the most numerous and powerful. The terrible small-pox and other epidemic diseases had not entered in among them, mowing them down by thousands, leaving them, as they are to-day, but a shadow or a wreck of their former glory. The most powerful chief among this tribe was called Maskepetoon, or "Crooked Arm," from the fact that one of his arms had been so hacked and wounded in his hand-to-hand conflicts with his neighbors, the Blackfeet Indians, that, in healing, the muscles had so contracted and stiffened that the arm remained crooked. He was a warlike chief, and his delight was in all the excitements of Indian conflicts, in cunning ambuscades, and, when successful, in the practice of unheard-of barbarities upon the captives of other tribes who fell into his hands. Very picturesque was the dress of many of these warriors of the plains. The quills of the eagle, which with them is considered the royal bird, formed the head-dress. Their shield was generally made of the tough leather of the neck of an old buffalo bull. The clothing, which was most elaborately ornamented and fringed, was made of the skins of the deer or moose, most beautifully tanned and prepared by the Indian women. Some of their horses were really magnificent animals, and marvelously trained for Indian warfare.

The Rev. Mr. Rundle, of the English Wesleyan Missionary Society, was the first missionary who at great personal risk visited the Cree tribes and faithfully declared the message of salvation to them. It was news indeed, and startled those wild prairie warriors; and the question went around among them, "Where did this little man come from with such strange tidings?" The conjurers were called upon to solve the question, and the answer was that he had come direct from Heaven wrapped in a large piece of paper.

The Rev. James Evans, also . . . visited Maskepetoon and faithfully preached to him and his people. Some accepted the truth and became Christians, but Maskepetoon was too fond of war to quickly receive the message of peace.

A number of years later the Rev. George McDougall went out, in prosecution of his missionary work, to those mighty plains, on one of which in after years he so mysteriously died. That he might be more successful in his efforts to bring them to Christ, Mr. McDougall frequently left his own home, and for months together lived with these red men as they wandered over vast stretches of country, hunting the buffalo and other game. His custom was always to have religious service every evening where they camped for the night. . . . At these camp-fire services hymns were sung, prayers were offered, and God's word was read and expounded. One evening Mr. McDougall read as his lesson the story of the trial and death of the Lord Jesus. He dwelt particularly upon the prayer of the Saviour for his murderers, "Father, forgive them, for they know not what they do," and, well aware of the Indian spirit of revenge that was so prominent in the hearts of his hearers, he dwelt strongly upon it, and plainly told them that if they really expected forgiveness from God, they must have the same mind that was in Christ, and forgive their enemies. Maskepetoon was observed to be deeply moved under the sermon, but nothing was said to him that evening. The next day, as the great company, consisting of many hundreds, was riding along over the beautiful prairies, an Indian chief rode quickly to the side of Mr. McDougall, and in quiet but excited tones asked him to fall back in the rear, as they did not wish him, the missionary, to witness the torture and killing of a man who was in that little band of Indians that was approaching them, although still so far away as to be almost indistinguishable to the eyes of a white man.

It seems that months before this Maskepetoon had sent his son across a mountain range or pass to bring from a sheltered valley a herd of horses which had there wintered. Very sublime and magnificent is some of the Rocky Mountain scenery. Travelers who have visited the Alps and other picturesque mountainous regions declare that some of the views in the Canadian "Rockies" are not excelled in any other part of the world. . . . Among the foot-hills of these mountains are many beautiful valleys, where the grass and herbage abound all the year, and it was in one of them that Maskepetoon had kept his reserved horses. He selected one of his warriors as his son's comrade to aid him in the work. From what afterward was found out it seems that the man, having a chance to sell the horses, his cupidity was excited, and so he murdered the chief's son, disposed of the horses, and hiding for the time his booty returned to the tribe with the plausible story that when they were coming across one of the dangerous passes in the mountains the young man lost his foothold and fell over one of the awful precipices, and was dashed to pieces, and that he alone was unable to manage the herd of horses, and so they had scattered on the plains.

Knowing nothing at the time to the contrary, Maskepetoon and his people were obliged to accept this story, improbable as it seemed. However, the truth came out after a while, for there had been, unknown to the murderer, witnesses of the tragedy. And now, for the first time since the truth had been revealed, the father was approaching the band in which was the murderer of his son. That the missionary might not see the dire vengeance that would be wreaked upon the culprit was the reason why this subordinate chief had requested Mr. McDougall to slacken his pace and fall into the rear of the crowd. Instead of doing so he quickened the speed of his horse and rode up to a position a little in the rear of the mighty chief, who, splendidly mounted, was leading the van of his warriors. On they galloped over the beautiful green sward, the missionary's heart uplifted in prayer that the wrath of man might be turned to the praise of God.

When the two bands approached within a few hundred yards of each other the eagle eye of the old warrior chief detected the murderer, and, drawing his tomahawk from his belt, he rode up until he was face to face with the man who had done him the greatest injury that it was possible to inflict upon him. Mr. McDougall, who still kept near enough to hear and see all that transpired, says that Maskepetoon, with a voice tremulous with suppressed feeling, and yet with an admirable command over himself, looking the man in the face who had nearly broken his heart, thus sternly addressed him: "You have murdered my boy, and you deserve to die. I picked you out as his trusted companion and gave you the post of honor as his comrade, and you have betrayed my trust and cruelly killed my only son. You have done me and the tribe the greatest injury possible for a man to do, for you have broken my heart and you have destroyed him who was to have succeeded me when I am not among the living. You deserve to die, and but for what I heard from the missionary last night at the campfire before this I would have buried this tomahawk in your brains. The missionary told us that if we expected to be forgiven, we must forgive our enemies, even those who had done us the greatest wrong. You have been my worst enemy, and you deserve to die." Then, in a voice tremulous with deepest emotion, he added, "As I hope to be forgiven, I forgive you." Then, speaking up sternly, he added, "But go immediately from among my people, and let me never see your face again." Then hastily pulling up his war-bonnet over his head his forced calmness gave way, and, quivering with the suppressed feelings that tore his heart, he bowed down over his horse's neck and gave way to an agony of tears.

Talk not of grief till thou hast seen
The tears of warlike men.

Maskepetoon lived for years afterward the life of a devoted, consistent Christian. All his old warlike habits were given up, and, mastering the syllabic characters in which the Cree Bible is printed, the word of God became his solace and his joy. He spent the remainder of his days in doing good. Very earnest and thrilling were the addresses which he gave to his own people as he urged them to give up all their old sinful ways and become followers of that Saviour who had so grandly saved him. Many listened to his words, and, like him, gave up their old warlike habits and settled down to quiet, peaceful lives. Anxious to benefit his old enemies, the Blackfeet, and to tell to them the story of the Saviour's love, he fearlessly and unarmed went among them with his Bible in his hand. A blood-thirsty chief of that tribe saw him coming, and, remembering some of their fierce conflicts of other days, and perhaps having lost by Maskepetoon's prowess some of his own relations in those conflicts, he seized his gun, and in defiance of all rules of humanity he coolly shot the converted Christian chieftain down.

Thus sadly fell Maskepetoon, a wondrous trophy of the cross, and one whose conversion did a vast amount of good, showing the power of the Gospel to change the hardest heart and to enable the warlike savage to conquer so thoroughly the besetting sin of the Indian character, even under the most extreme provocation, where very few indeed could have found fault if the price of blood had been exacted and the murderer summarily executed.[1]

END NOTES

One—A Medicine Man's Daughter

1. John Chaput, "The Frog Lake Massacre" (*The Encyclopedia of Saskatchewan*, http://esask.uregina.ca/entry/frog_lake_massacre.html.
2. "Intergenerational Impacts" (Legacy of Hope Foundation, Ottawa, ON: http://www.wherearethechildren.ca/en/exhibit/impacts.html).

Two—Religious Influences

1. Information taken from an online edition of *Strong's Concordance* (http://www.eliyah.com/lexicon.html).

Five—Satan's False Gospel

1. See 2 Corinthians 11:3; 13–15; 1 John 4:1–3; Acts 20:29; Revelation 13:11–14.

Six—New Age Elements in Native Spirituality

1. A definition given to my publisher by Sarah Leslie of Discernment Research Group (http://herescope.blogspot.com).
2. Ray Yungen, "Has the New Age Infiltrated Christianity" (http://www.lighthousetrailsresearch.com/newage.htm).
3. Ray Yungen, *For Many Shall Come in My Name* (Eureka, MT: Lighthouse Trails Publishing, 2nd ed. 2007), p. 16.
4. *Encarta World English Dictionary* (Microsoft Corporation, 1998-2005, http://encarta.msn.com/encnet/features/dictionary/ dictionaryhome.aspx).
5. Alexander, Brooks. *Witchcraft Goes Mainstream: Uncovering Its Alarming Impact on You and Your Family* (Eugene, OR: Harvest House, 2004), p. 33.
6. Berit Kjos, *Under the Spell of Mother Earth* (Kjos Ministries, http://www.crossroad.to/Books/UnderSpell/4-Witchcraft&Ecology.htm), ch. 4.
7. Ibid.
8. Website on North American Indians (http://www.scribd.com/doc/5025401/Ancient-Religions).
9. Indian Bible College, "A Biblical Position by Native Leaders on

Native Spirituality" (Flaggstaff, AZ, http://www.indianbible.org/about-us/spiritualism.html).

10. Matthew Fox, *The Coming of the Cosmic Christ* (New York, NY: HarperCollins Publishers, 1980), p. 154.

11. See Lighthouse Trails Research for extensive research on these topics (http://www.lighthousetrailsresearch.com).

12. Cliff Schaeffer, Unpublished manuscript, p. 45.

13. 2 Corinthians 5:17.

14. From unpublished manuscript by Cliff Schaeffer, section called "What Do These Animal Spirits Represent?," p. 51.

15. Indian Bible College, "A Biblical Position by Native Leaders on Native Spirituality," op. cit.

16. See the article "Shamanism in the Church: Occult 'Eagle Spirituality' Manifests in Popular 'Prophetic' Ministries" by Mark Dinsmore (http://www.thebereancall.org/node/2682).

17. Berit Kjos, *Brave New Schools (*Kjos Ministries, http://www.crossroad.to/Books/BraveNewSchools/1-globalvillage.html), ch. 1.

18. "The Medicine Wheel" by Francis Whiskeyjack (http://web.archive.org/web/20100412122830/http://www.ammsa.com/buffalo-spirit/June-2000/medicinewheel.html).

19. Cliff Schaeffer, "A Biblical Look at Native Spiritualism" (http://hisriches.com/hisriches/articles/a-biblical-look-at-native-spiritualism).

20. Larry DeBruyn, "Spiritualism's Slippery Slope" (Herescope blog: http://herescope.blogspot.com/2012/01/spiritualisms-slippery-slope.html), part 5 of the book review of Steve Berger's book, *Have Heart.*

21. Huston Smith and Reuben Snake, *One Nation Under God: The Triumph of the Native American Church* (Sante Fe, NM: Clear Light Publishers, eds., 1996), pp. 167-173; (Quoted from University of Virginia Religious Movements (http://web.archive.org/web/20060829153914/http://religiousmovements.lib.virginia.edu/nrms/naspirit.html).

22. Edward F. Anderson, *Peyote: The Divine Cactus,* (Tucson, AZ: The University of Arizona Press 1980), p. 41; (Quoted from University of Virginia Religious Movements: http://web.archive.org/web/20060829153914/http://religiousmovements.lib.virginia.edu/nrms/naspirit.html).

23. University of Virginia Religious Movements: "Native American Spirituality" (http://web.archive.org/web/20060829153914/http://religiousmovements.lib.virginia.edu/nrms/naspirit.html).

24. Jay Fikes, "A Brief History of the Native American Church"

(http://csp.org/communities//docs/fikes-nac_history.html).

25. Thomas Merton stated this to mystic Matthew Fox. Fox talked about this in an interview (http://web.archive.org/web/20060425035122/nineoclockservice.tripod.com/mattiefx.htm).

26. Maureen Grace Burns, "Native American Sacred Hoop Visionquest—Sacred Pipe Ceremony and Powwows" (http://web.archive.org/web/20090211103210/http://blessingscornucopia.com/Native_American_Indian_Sacred_Hoop_Visionquest_Sacred_Pipe_Ceremony_and_Powwows.htm).

27. Cliff Schaeffer, "A Biblical Look at Native Spiritualism," op. cit.

28. See Ray Yungen's article "Understanding the Spirituality of Sue Monk Kidd" (http://www.lighthousetrailsresearch.com/blog/?p=942).

29. There is extensive research and documentation on Kjos Ministries website about Mother Earth, goddess spirituality, and earth-based spirituality (http://www.crossroad.to).

30. *Merriam-Webster's Dictionary*, online edition (http://www.merriam-webster.com/dictionary/potlatch).

31. Taken from Wikipedia (http://en.wikipedia.org/wiki/Potlatch).

32. Duane Champange, *Contemporary Native American Cultural Issues* (Walnut Creek, CA : AltaMira Press, 1999), p. 141.

33. Maureen Grace Burns,"Native American Sacred Hoop Visionquest—Drumming Smudging and Sweat Lodges" (http://web.archive.org/web/20090211111034/http://blessingscornucopia.com/Native_American_Indian_Sacred_Hoop_Visionquest_Drumming_Smudging_and_Sweat_Lodges.htm).

34. Larry Zimmerman, *Native North America (Civilization of the American Indian)* (Great Britain: Duncan Baird Publishers, 1996), p. 90.

35. John Ankerberg and John Weldon, *Encyclopedia of New Age Beliefs* (Eugene, OR: Harvest House, 1996); (taken from http://www.ankerberg.org/Articles/_PDFArchives/new-age/NA3W0801.pdf).

36. John P. Newport, *The New Age Movement and the Biblical Worldview* (Grand Rapids, MI: Eerdman's Publishing Co, 1998), p. 34.

37. John Ankerberg, John Weldon, Ankerberg Theological Research Institute (http://www.ankerberg.org/Articles/archives-na.htm, scroll down page to section on Shamanism - 8 parts).

38. "Kundalini, Short Circuits, Risks, and Information" (http://kundalini.se/eng/engkni_1024.html).

39. John Ankerberg, John Weldon (Ankerberg Theological Research

Institute, http://www.ankerberg.org/Articles/archives-na.htm) quoted from Joan Halifax, *Shamanic Voices*, (New York, NY: Penguin, 1979), pp. 7-27.

40. Sandy Simpson, "The Elijah List" (http://www.letusreason.org/Latrain36.htm).

41. Larry Zimmerman, *Native North America*, op. cit., p. 99.

42. To understand more about the Catholic eucharist and transubstantiation, read "The New Evangelization and the Coming Eucharistic Christ" by Roger Oakland (http://www.understandthetimes.org/commentary/c47.shtml) and *Another Jesus* by Roger Oakland.

43. Cliff Schaeffer, "A Biblical Look at Native Spiritualism," op. cit.,

44. Larry Zimmerman, *Native North America*, op. cit., p. 99.

45. Ibid.

Seven—False Christs, Plastic Shamans, & Mother Earth

1. Paul Bailey, *Ghost Dance Messiah* (New York, NY: Tower Publications, Inc., MCMLXX), p. 12.

2. Ibid, back cover.

3. Ibid, pp. 5-6.

4. Ibid, p. 6.

5. To understand certain aspects of "earth spirituality" or earth-based spirituality, read "Is Earth Our Mother?" by Berit Kjos (http://www.crossroad.to/Books/UnderSpell/1-Earth.htm).

6. "Native American Spirituality" (University of Virginia, New Religious Movements project: http://web.archive.org/web/20060830091802/http://religiousmovements.lib.virginia.edu/nrms/naspirit.htmlon).

7. "1923—1950: The Williams Treaties and Land Transfer Agreements" (Canada in the Making, Aboriginals: Treaties & Relations, http://www.canadiana.ca/citm/themes/aboriginals/aboriginals11_e.html).

8. "Native American Spirituality" (Ontario Consultants on Religious Tolerance, http://www.religioustolerance.org/nataspir.htm).

9. "Canadian Charter of Rights and Freedoms" (Department of Justice, Canada. http://laws.justice.gc.ca/en/charter/#libertes).

10. "Native American Spirituality," Ontario Consultants on Religious Tolerance, op. cit.

11. For more information on Pan Indianism, see: http://en.wikipedia.org/wiki/Pan-Indianism.

12. "Native American Spirituality," Ontario Consultants on Religious Tolerance, op. cit.

13. Wilmer Stampede Mesteth, et al., "Declaration of war against exploiters of Lakota Spirituality" (http://puffin.creighton.edu/lakota/war.html and "Responses to the Declaration: War against exploiters of Lakota Spirituality," http://puffin.creighton.edu/lakota/war_4.html).
14. Ibid.
15. Read Geary Hobson's book *The Remembered Earth*, pp. 100-108 in the section titled: "The Rise of the White Shaman as a New Version of Cultural Imperialism" about plastic shamanism.
16. "Plastic Shaman (http://www.nationmaster.com/encyclopedia/Plastic-shaman).
17. Lloyd Grove, "Oprah and the Sweat Lodge Guru" (The Daily Beast, October 23, 2009, http://www.thedailybeast.com/articles/2009/10/23/oprah-and-the-sweat-lodge-guru.html).
18. Sachem Walkingfox, "Who is Smudging and Why?" (http://walkingfox.tripod.com/id9.html).
19. The testimony of former shaman, Donald Holsclaw. Used with permission.
20. For more information on Shoefoot, read The Berean Call's article: "The Spirit Lie" (http://www.thebereancall.org/node/2591).
21. Jonathan Wachtel, "U.N. Prepares to Debate Whether 'Mother Earth' Deserves Human Rights Status" (Fox News, April 18, 2011, http://www.foxnews.com/world/2011/04/18/prepares-debate-rights-mother-earth/#ixzz1qqbFteLN www.foxnews.com/world/2011/04/18/prepares-debate-rights-mother-earth).
22. Ibid.
23. Carl Teichrib, "Uniting Religions for World Change: The G8 World Religions Summit" (Forcing Change, article on Kjos Ministries website, http://www.crossroad.to/articles2/forcing-change/010/6-world-religions-summit.htm).
24. Ibid.
25. For more information about Rick Warren's global P.E.A.C.E. Plan, visit http://www.lightousetrailsresearch.com/peaceplan.htm.
26. Roger Oakland, *Faith Undone* (Eureka, MT: Lighthouse Trails Publishing, 2007), pp. 147-149.
27. "Manitoba's Native leaders see a return to ancient traditions and spiritual values as the solution to modern problems" (Radio Canada International, February 6, 2012, http://www.rcinet.ca/english/column/the-link-s-top-stories/15-48_2012-02-06-manitobarsquo-s-native-

leaders-see-a-return-to-ancient-traditions-and-spiritual-values-as-the-solution-to-modern-problems).

28. Used *The Free Dictionary* (http://www.thefreedictionary.com), Merriam-Webster (http://www.merriam-webster.com/dictionary/), and Dictionary.com (http://dictionary.reference.com/browse) plus referred to Deuteronomy and the Hebrew concordance for these definitions.

Eight—Native Spirituality & the Emerging Church

1. Lance Dickie, "The Pull of History and Healing" (*The Seattle Times*, July 27, 2007, http://seattletimes.nwsource.com/html/opinion/2003807813_lance27.html).

2. Lumni Nation (http://www.whatcomvolunteer.org/HOC__Organization_Profile_Page?Oid=0018000000t9HvPAAU).

3. Richard Twiss, *One Church Many Tribes* (Ventura, CA: Regal Books from Gospel Light, 2000), pp. 20-21.

4. Ibid., p. 21.

5. For an excellent article on contemporary feminism and goddess worship, see Berit Kjos' "Welcoming the Goddess," chapter 5 from her book, *Under the Spell of Mother Earth* (online at http://www.crossroad.to/Books/ UnderSpell/5-goddess.htm). The chapter also features an informative chart, "Common Practices of Earth-Centered Religions," which shows the common practices of pagan religions: trance states, dreams and visions, divination, spiritism, magic/sorcery, charms/amulets, solstice rites, serpent worship, and sacred sex.

6. There is an excellent article about earth-based spirituality called "Native, Indigenous, and Nature Religion" from Dave Hunt's book, *Occult Invasion* (ch. 8, online at http://www.ankerberg.com/Articles/new-age/NA0201W2.htm).

7. See "Al Gore's Vision of Global Salvation: Quotations from his 1992 best-seller: *Earth in the Balance*" by Berit Kjos (http://www.crossroad. to/text/articles/Gore7-99.html).

8. Philip Jenkins, *Dream Catchers: How mainstream America discovered Native Spirituality* (New York, NY: Oxford University Press, 2004), p. 5.

9. Bill Glen, "Catholic School Makes Room for Native Spirituality" (*Western Catholic Reporter*, November 6, 2006, http://wcr.ab.ca/old-site/news/2006/1106/bencalf110606.shtml).

10. Ibid.

11. Ibid.

12. Ibid.

13. Pamela Sexsmith, "Native Spirituality Celebrated in Catholic School System" (The Aboriginal Multi-Media Society, 2006, Vol. 4, Issue 5, http://www.ammsa.com/node/14133).

14. Pat Walsh, "In Montana a Novice Finds 'a Beautiful Marriage Between Catholic and Native Spirituality'" (*News of the Northwest Jesuits*, Spring 2008, http://www.nwjesuits.info/news/index.php?option=com_content&view=article&id=32:in-montana-a-novice-finds-a-beautiful-marriage-between-catholic-and-native-spirituality&catid=8:vocations-a-formation&Itemid=14).

15. Ibid.

16. Mennonite Church Canada website's Resource Centre (http://www.mennonitechurch.ca/resourcecentre/ResourceView/5/10786?useref=0).

17. Ibid.

18. Michael L. Cooper-White, "Dream Catchers: The ELCA Commission for Women" (*Lutheran Woman Today,* March 2004, http://www.lutheranwomantoday.org/back/04issues/0304article3.html).

19. Mark Batterson, *The Circle Maker* (Grand Rapids, MI: Zondervan, http://thecirclemaker.com/images/wk1.jpg), pp. 9-10.

20. Ibid.

21. Richard Twiss, *One Church Many Tribes,* op. cit., p. 23.

22. Ibid.

23. Ibid., pp. 132-133.

24. Ibid., p. 133.

25. Emergent Village Theological Conference, http://iowaemergent.blogspot.com/2010/11/emergent-village-theological-conference.html

26. RichardTwiss, *One Church Many Tribes*, op. cit., p. 92.

27. Ibid., p. 91.

28. For more information on Rob Bell's Everything is Spiritual tour, see the DVD *Quantum Lie* with Warren B. Smith and Bob DeWaay at www.lighthousetrails.com.

29. Richard Twiss, *One Church Many Tribes*, op. cit., p. 93.

30. Ray Yungen, *A Time of Departing* (Eureka, MT: Lighthouse Trails Publishing, 2nd ed. 2006), pp. 108-109).

31. Neale Donald Walsch, *The New Revelations* (New York, NY: Atria Books, 2002), pp. 175, 157; as quoted from *Deceived on Purpose* by Warren B. Smith (Magalia, CA: Mountain Stream Press, 2nd edition,

3rd printing), pp. 61-62.

32. A Preamble by CHIEF, Inc, "A Biblical Position by Native Leaders on Native Spirituality" (1998: http://chief.org/about-2/a-biblical-position-on-native-spirituality).

33. Indian Bible College, "A Biblical Position by Native Leaders on Native Spirituality, op. cit.

34. Trevor Persaud, "Sweat Lodge Prayers" (*Christianity Today*, April 13, 2011, http://www.christianitytoday.com/ct/2011/april/sweatlodgeprayers.html).

35. Annette Francis, "Banned Sweat Lodge" (APTN National News, January 17, 2011, http://www.newagefraud.org/smf/index.php?topic=3125.0;wap2#ixzz1njuMGAZ1).

Nine—Can Cultures Be Redeemed?

1. Sandy Simpson, Deception in the Church, "Reasons to Reject the "World Christian Gathering on Indigenous People" Movement" (http://www.deceptioninthechurch.com/reasonstoreject.html).

2. Mike Oppenheimer, "Culturizing Christianity" (http://www.letusreason.org/current70.htm).

3. *Random House Dictionary*, taken from Let Us Reason website: "Looking For God in All the Wrong Places" (http://www.letusreason.org/Emerge13.htm).

4. Mike Oppenheimer, "Culturizing Christianity" (http://www.letusreason.org/current70.htm).

5. Ibid.

6. YWAM, Island Breeze Training, "What is a Discipleship Training School?" (http://web.archive.org/web/20070712212212/http://www.islandbreeze.com.au/training.htm).

7. Leon Siu, Aloha Ke Akua, Word to the World with host Danny Lehmann, KLHT, 2001, show #544, courtesy Sandy Simpson, Deception in the Church who transcribed this program.

8. Aloha Ke Akua Ministries (http://akaministries.tripod.com/aloha).

9. Sandy Simpson, "Reasons to Reject the 'World Christian Gathering on Indigenous People' Movement" (March 2006, http://www.deceptioninthechurch.com/reasonstoreject.html).

10. Discernment Research Group, "The Indigenous People's Movement" (August 2, 2007, http://herescope.blogspot.com/2007/08/

indigenous-peoples-movement.html).

11. Daniel Kikawa, *Perpetuated in Righteousness* (Aloha Ke Akua Pub; 4th edition, 1994), p. 27.

12. Aloha Ke Akua "Books" page (http://akaministries.tripod.com/aloha/id3.html).

13. Mike Oppenheimer, "Culturizing Christianity," op. cit.

14. Sandy Simpson, "Reasons to Reject the 'World Christian Gathering on Indigenous People' Movement," op. cit.

15. Ibid.

16. Ibid.

17. Ibid.

18. Mike Oppenheimer, "Culturizing Christianity," op. cit.

19. Terry LeBlanc, Word to the World program #542, as cited by Mike Oppenheimer, "Culturizing Christianity," op. cit.

20. Nanci Des Gerlaise, from the foreword of *Stories From Indian Wigwams and Northern Campfires* (Eureka, MT: Lighthouse Trails Publishing, 2011).

21. Titus Coan, Missionary to Hawaii (http://www.path2prayer.com/article/1051/revival-and-holy-spirit/books-sermons/new-resources/famous-christians-books-and-sermons/titus-coan-missionary-to-hawaii).

22. Amy Dueckman,"Listening Circle Brings Together Two Cultures" (*Intotemak*, Mennonite Church Canada, Summer 2006, Vol. 35, No. 2, www.mennonitechurch.ca/files/news/intotemak/intotemakv35n2.pdf).

23. Discernment Research Group, "The Newest Heresy of the NAR: Orality" (Herescope blog, March 8th, 2006 (http://herescope.blogspot.com/2006/03/newest-heresy-of-nar-orality.html).

24. Amy Dueckman,"Listening Circle Brings Together Two Cultures," op. cit.

25. A Symposium on Progressive Christianity; A Patheos Symposium hosted by the Patheos Progressive Christian Portal, in partnership with the Wild Goose Festival (interview at http://www.progressive-christianalliance.org/Blog/articles/rev-jarrod-cochrans-interview-with-patheos.)

Ten—Living Water

1. "Suicide, Murder, and Death in the Occult," Part 1 of a two-part series by Dr. John Ankerberg and Dr. John Weldon (http://www.

ankerberg. org/Articles/archives-na.htm).

2. Ephesians 6:10–18: "Finally, my brethren, be strong in the Lord, and in the power of his might. Put on the whole armour of God, that ye may be able to stand against the wiles of the devil. For we wrestle not against flesh and blood, but against principalities, against powers, against the rulers of the darkness of this world, against spiritual wickedness in high places. Wherefore take unto you the whole armour of God, that ye may be able to withstand in the evil day, and having done all, to stand. Stand therefore, having your loins girt about with truth, and having on the breastplate of righteousness; And your feet shod with the preparation of the gospel of peace; Above all, taking the shield of faith, wherewith ye shall be able to quench all the fiery darts of the wicked. And take the helmet of salvation, and the sword of the Spirit, which is the word of God: Praying always with all prayer and supplication in the Spirit, and watching thereunto with all perseverance and supplication for all saints."

3. The bulk of this prayer for the armor of God is quoted from the book *The Dark Side of Karate* by Linda Nathan and Tonie Gatlin. (1st Book Library, 2003), used with permission.

Terminology

1. Definitions from Aboriginal Affairs and Northern Development Canada (http://www.aadnc-aandc.gc.ca/eng/1100100010002).

Appendix II—The Names for God

1. Most of the research to compile this list of names for God comes from the following websites: http://www.blueletterbible.org, http://www.eliyah.com/strongs.htm, http://smilegodlovesyou.org/names.html, http://heavenawaits.com/biblestudies/names.html, http://www.breadoflifebiblestudy.com.

Appendix III—The Story of Maskepetoon

1. Egerton Ryerson Young, *Stories From Indian Wigwams and Northern Campfires* (Eureka, MT: Lighthouse Trails Publishing, 2010), pp. 108-114.

Photos and Illustrations Credits

Page 8: Cree Camp on the prairie, south of Vermilion, Alberta. September 1871. By Charles Horetzky (1838 - 1900), public domain.

Page 24 (top): Portrait of Native students at St. Paul's Indian Industrial School, Middlechurch, Manitoba, 1901; used with permission from Library and Archives Canada, item number P-182251, Mikan number 3354514; (bottom): Aboriginal children in class at the Roman Catholic-run Fort George Catholic Indian Residential School, Fort George, Quebec, 1939, used with permission by Archives Deschâtelets, Ottawa, ON.

Page 25: Aboriginal students and staff assembled outside the Kamloops Indian Residential School, Kamloops, British Columbia, 1934 used with permission by Archives Deschâtelets, Ottawa, ON.

Page 84: Medicine Wheel, photo from www.bigstockphoto.com; used with permission.

Page 91: Quanah Parker, a Kwahadi Comanche chief; full-length, standing in front of tent. Photographed by Lanney, 116-SC-87722, public domain, used with permission from National Archives.

Page 104: Little Big Mouth, a medicine man, seated in front of his lodge near Fort Sill, Oklahoma, with medicine bag visible from behind the tent. Photographed by William S. Soule, 1869-70, 075-OBE-1448D, public domain, used with permission from National Archives.

Page 113: Jack Wilson "Wovoka," public domain.

Page 160: Chichen Itza—the ancient ziggurat of chichen itza at mexico; photo from www.bigstockphoto.com; used with permission.

INDEX

A

Note: Certain words, like Native Spirituality or God, appear so frequently in the book that they are not included in this Index.

E

F

N

For Further Study

Books

Idolatry in Their Hearts by Mike Oppenheimer and Sandy Simpson
www.letusreason.org
The Other Side of the River by Kevin Reeves
www.lighthousetrails.com
Under the Spell of Mother Earth by Berit Kjos
www.crossroad.to
Faith Undone: the emerging church—a new reformation or an endtime deception by Roger Oakland
www.lighthousetrails.com
A Time of Departing by Ray Yungen
www.lighthousetrails.com

DVDs/Videos

"I'll Never God Back!—The testimony of Chief Shoefoot, a former shaman
www.lighthousetrails.com
The First Nations Movement: Deceiving the Nations
with Mike Oppenheimer and Sandy Simpson
www.lighthousetrails.com
The Submerging Church with Joe Schimmel
www.lighthousetrails.com

Websites:

www.nancidesgerlaise.com—Nanci Des Gerlaise's website
www.lighthousetrailsresearch.com—Lighthouse Trails Research Project
www.crossroad.to—Kjos Ministries
www.letusreason.org—Let Us Reason Ministries
www.deceptioninthechurch.com—Deception in the Church
www.understandthetimes.org—Understand the Times
www.thebereancall.org—The Berean Call
www.spiritual-research-network.com—Spiritual Research Network

Other Products by Lighthouse Trails Publishing

BOOKS

Another Jesus (2nd ed.), by Roger Oakland, $12.95

A Time of Departing, 2nd ed., by Ray Yungen, $13.95

Castles in the Sand (a novel), by Carolyn A. Greene, $12.95

Dangerous Illusions (sequel to *Castles in the Sand*), by Carolyn A. Greene and Zach Taylor, $14.95

Faith Undone, by Roger Oakland, $13.95

For Many Shall Come in My Name (2nd ed.) by Ray Yungen, $13.95

Foxe's Book of Martyrs, by John Foxe, $14.95, illustrated

How to Prepare for Hard Times and Persecution, by Maria Kneas, $13.95

How to Protect Your Child from the New Age & Spiritual Deception, by Berit Kjos, $14.95

Let There Be Light, by Roger Oakland, 2nd ed., $13.95

Stolen from My Arms, by Katherine Sapienza, $14.95

Stories from Indian Wigwams and Northern Campfires, by Egerton Ryerson Young, $15.95

Egerton Ryerson Young
$15.95, illustrated, photos

Strength for Tough Times, by Maria Kneas, $7.95

The Color of Pain, by Gregory Reid, $10.95

Things We Couldn't Say, by Diet Eman, $14.95, photos

The Other Side of the River by Kevin Reeves, $13.95

Trapped in Hitler's Hell, by Anita Dittman with Jan Markell
$13.95, illustrated, photos

DVDs

The Story of Anita Dittman with Anita Dittman
$15.95, 60 minutes

The New Face of Mystical Spirituality with Ray Yungen
3-DVDs, $39.95 or $14.95 ea.

The Emerging Church lecture series (4 DVDs), by Roger Oakland, $49.95

For a complete listing of all our books and DVDs, go to www.lighthousetrails.com, or request a copy of our catalog.

To order additional copies of:

MUDDY WATERS

Send $14.95 per book

plus shipping (USA: $5.00 flat rate shipping) to:

Lighthouse Trails Publishing
P.O. Box 908
Eureka, MT 59917

Call or go online for information about quantity discounts.

You may order online at
www.lighthousetrails.com
or
Call our toll-free order number:
866/876-3910 (USA & Canada order line)

For all other calls, including all international calls:
406/889-3610
Fax: 406/889-3633

Muddy Waters, as well as other books by Lighthouse Trails Publishing, can be ordered through all major outlet stores, bookstores, online bookstores, and Christian bookstores.

Bookstores may order through:
Ingram, SpringArbor, Anchor,
or directly through Lighthouse Trails.
Libraries may order through Baker & Taylor.

Quantity discounts available for most of our books.
International orders may be placed either online, by phone, through e-mail, or by faxing or mailing order form.

For other biblically based products you can trust:
www.lighthousetrails.com

Made in the USA
Columbia, SC
13 September 2018